For The Love Of Children

A *Guidebook* For Early Childhood Education

International, Third Edition

Compiled By

Marguerite Laskares, Tamra Pace, Vanessa Conaway Pace

Illustrated By

Marguerite Laskares

Poetry By

Vanessa Conaway Pace

Pace Publishing International, Post Office Box 2187, Lynnwood, WA 98036

For The Love Of Children

A *Guidebook* For Early Childhood (International Edition)

Compiled By: Marguerite Laskares, Tamra Pace, Vanessa Conaway Pace

Computer Expertise Provided By: Emerald-Forest Computer Services
                                  www.emerald-forest.net

Cover Design By: The Creative YOU!

ISBN Number: ISBN-13: 978-0-9704373-5-8
               ISBN-10: 0-9704373-5-8

First Edition Copyright © 2000 By: Pace Publishing International
Second Edition Copyright © 2012 By: Pace Publishing International
Third Edition Copyright © 2019 By   Pace Publishing International

                        Post Office Box 2187
                        Lynnwood, WA 98036 USA
                        www.fortheloveofchildrenbook.com
                        E-mail: info@.fortheloveofchildrenbook.com

Printed in the United States of America. All rights reserved under International Copyright Law. No part of these contents and/or cover may be reproduced in whole or in part in any form or by any means—electronic, mechanical, photocopy, video or audio recording, or any other—except for brief quotations in printed reviews, without the prior express written consent of the Publisher.

Dedicated to

Helen Laskares

Faithful Mother and Friend
Who has dedicated her life
To the training of her own children
And the children in her care.

Children of the World

We heard the cries
    Of those who dreamed
        About a better world,
           And knew
                That You
                    Must play
                        Your part
                            As that new world
                                Unfurled.

And so, we offer up
    Some thoughts
        To help them
            Help You grow
                So You
                    Can help them
                        Build the world
                            That we all
                                Want to know.

Vanessa Conaway Pace

Dear Children of the World,

We send this book to you with much love. It was compiled for those who care for you. Maybe this little book will enable them to make your young days happier and more comfortable. Maybe this little book will encourage your teachers and all your caregivers to continue in their most precious

vocation of serving and caring for you. If so this little book has accomplished its purpose.

Marguerite Laskares   Tamra Pace   Vanessa Pace

Teachers and Caregivers

We come to share
    Some messages
        That we,
            From life,
                Have learned
                    About how children
                        Learn and grow, ...

                          ... Its knowledge
                              We have **learned!**

We gleaned some
    From the books we've read,
        And classes we enjoyed,
            But most of all,
                We GREW them
                    In the schools
                        Where we deployed.

                                            Vanessa Conaway Pace

Dear Teachers and Caregivers,

Compiling this Guidebook has provided us a wonderful opportunity. It has given us a chance to share with you ideas and activities for young children. It has also given us the opportunity of asking you to share your ideas and activities with us.

Let us continue in our love and care for our "Little Ones."

Respectfully,

Marguerite Laskares   Tarmra Pace   Vanessa Pace

Learning By Experience

Reading about
    The things
        That others
            Did with their own hands,
                Won't make
                    <u>Your</u> muscles
                        Stronger,
                            Or help implement
                                <u>Your</u> plans.

For there's nothing like
    The feeling,
        When you've built it
            By yourself,
                And you're
                    Confident
                      That the skills
                        You've learned
                          Are stored within
                            <u>Your</u> shelf!!

Vanessa Conaway Pace

Reading about, or hearing about the experiences of others lets you know that <u>someone else</u> can do it, but, <u>experiencing</u> it lets you know that <u>you can do it</u>!

When I was a child my Father and Mother decided to build a chicken house on our farm. Days were exciting to me as WE planned the exact location for the building, set the sticks in the ground and tied strings to them so we would dig a straight foundation. Digging the trench by hand didn't even seem difficult to my young way of thinking because there was an air of excitement. WE were building a building!

Daddy let me help at every stage of the building process. WE hauled dirt away, then filled the returning wheelbarrows with little rocks to make the base of the footer. Then WE mixed cement and poured the foundation. As a reward I got to roller skate around and around on the dried cement,...at least until the tiles arrived for the walls!

Every day WE mixed more cement, and laid more rows of tiles. WE decided where the windows and doors would be, and measured how many tiles we would have to leave out to make the space for them. I learned how to use a level to make sure the walls would be even and straight, and how to brush the almost-dry cement in the joints so it would be nice and smooth.

As the days went on, and the rows of tiles became higher and higher, wonder of wonders, I could no longer see over the top of them. It began to feel as if I were inside a *real building*,...and I had helped build it with my own hands!!

The next year WE added another room onto our house. WE measured, and dug, and poured, and built. This time the building principles were the same, but more complicated and refined. *People* need more elaborate houses than chickens!! Again I got to roller skate on the new foundation, and dance on the sparkling new hardwood floors! I helped Daddy put the electrical wiring in, and Mother choose the colors and paint the walls and make curtains. It was all very exciting for my young life, and the whole experience nurtured that innate creative urge that exists in every child.

Now *I know* it can be done! Even better, I have a working knowledge of how to do it because I have done it with my own hands. As a result of these early childhood practical experiences I have the confidence and basic skills needed to undertake any creative or *re-creative* project. Having done it once, I can always do that, or any similar project, again

The same experiences were true for cooking, cleaning, sewing, designing clothes, designing and creating tools and equipment for our projects, building roads, planting gardens, teaching classes, typing papers, writing books, etc. In the actual *doing* of the project we often found that we had to turn to books and libraries to research our subject in more detail. Our hands-on experience inspired us to learn. What we *practiced and did* in small hands-on projects as children, we are able to do more successfully on a larger scale as adults.

Having personally seen how much practical, hands-on experiences have enriched my life, my hope is that the projects included in this *Guidebook* will help you enrich the lives of your children through *learning from experience*.

Vanessa Conaway Pace
Seattle, WA May 2000

Table of Contents

There's something here
    For everyone
        To get
            The job
                Of Teaching
                    Done!!!

So, choose the topic
    For today
        And start out running
            On your way
                To find
                    The answers
                        That you need,

Or, find a Lesson Plan
        With speed!

                      Vanessa Conaway Pace

Table of Contents

Frontispiece
Dedication
Introduction

"Dear Children of The World"..5
"Dear Teachers and Caregivers"...7
"Learning from Experience"...9
Table of Contents...11

Development Unit

The Absorbent Mind..21
Teachers/Caregivers: Inner Preparation...25
Teachers/Caregivers: Guidance Suggestions...28
Environment: A Classroom Planned for Learning....................................33
Environment: How To Start A Classroom..34
Children: Ages and Stages: Birth To One Year..35
Children: Ages and Stages: One To Two Years.......................................38
Children: Ages and Stages: Two Years To Three Years..........................40
Children: Ages and Stages: Three-Year-Olds..42
Children: Ages and Stages: Four-Year-Olds..44
Children: Ages and Stages: Five-Year-Olds...46

Part I: Gathering Time/Circle Time

Introduction To Gathering Time/Circle Time..49
   Gathering Time/Circle Time Expectations...51
   Gathering Times - When   - Why...52
      1. Presentation of Games and Activities: General Points...............53
      2. Example of Group Presentation: Handling a Book......................54
Skills To Develop..55
Activities - Overview..55
Equipment...55
Objectives..55
Ideas for Room Arrangement...56
More Activities..56
Concepts - Preschool Level..57

Part 2: Growing Exercises

Introduction To Growing Exercises...61
    The Benefits of Preschool Cookery: Science..............................62
    The Benefits of Preschool Cookery: Language Stimulation........63
    Recipe For A Happy Day..63
Skills To Develop..64
Activities – Overview..64
Equipment..64
Objectives..64
Ideas for Room Arrangement..65
More Activities..65
More Growing Exercises...66
    1.   Care of Person: Grooming..66
    2.   Care of Person: Dressing..67
    3.   Care of Environment: Sweeping...................................68
    4.   Care of Environment: Dusting......................................69
    5.   Plant and Garden Care: Flower Arranging................70
    6.   Plant and Garden Care: The Garden..........................72
    7.   General Growing Exercises: Managing Plastic Food Containers.74
    8.   General Growing Exercises: Managing Bottles with Screw Tops.75
    9.   General Growing Exercises: Managing "Squeeze" Containers.....76
    10. General Growing Exercises: Learning To Use a Spoon................77
    11. General Growing Exercises: Pouring...78
    12. General Growing Exercises: Dry Measure – Spoons....................79
    13. General Growing Exercises: Liquid/Dry Measure Containers.....80
Cooking Recipes...81
Extended Growing Exercises (For Older Children)........................83
    1.   Dressing..83
    2.   Care of Clothing..83
    3.   Grooming...83
    4.   Care of Environment..84
    5.   Plant and Garden Care..85
    6.   Food Preparation...85
    7.   Feeding Self..86
    8.   Fine Hand Development...86

Part 3: Science

Introduction To Science...91
    Noticing...91

On-Going Nature Collection		91
Science Scrapbook		92
Sensory Perception		92
Sorting		92
Testing		92
Labeling		93
Changes		93
Spontaneous versus Planned Science		94
What To Present		94
Teaching Strategies		94
Role of the Teacher		95

Skills To Develop 96
Activities - Overview 96
Equipment 96
Objectives 96
Ideas for Room Arrangement 97
More Activities 97
Science Projects 98

1. Animal, Bird, or Fish 98
2. Nature Hunt 99
3. How Big Is a STICK? 100
4. Flower Arranging 102
5. Long Planter Box or Small Garden Spot 103
6. Is It Full? 104
7. Sink and Float 105
8. Rope Knowledge 106
9. Balance Board 107
10. Weighing Game 108
11. Weather: What Makes the Rain? 109
12. Weather: Air Contains Water 110
13. Weather: Evaporation 111
14. Weather: What Makes Lightning? 113
15. Weather: What Makes Thunder? 114
16. Weather: What Makes a Rainbow? 115
17. Weather: Wind 117
18. Seeds 118
19. Plants: From Seed To Flower/Life Cycle of a Plant ... 119
20. Plant Parts: Flowers/Vegetables 120
21. Flower Identification 121
22. Insect Information 122

Part 4: Mathematics

Introduction To Mathematics	127
Skills To Develop	128
Activities - Overview	128
Equipment	128
Objectives	128
Ideas for Room Arrangement	129
More Activities	129
1. Free Exploration: Treasure Boxes	130
2. Free Exploration: Treasure Pattern Cards	131
3. Patterns: Rhythmic Clapping	132
4. Patterns: The Dot Chart	133
5. Patterns: Dot Chart Patterns	134
6. Patterns: People Row Patterns	135
7. Sorting and Classifying: Treasure Boxes	136
8. Sorting and Classifying: Walks	137
9. Counting: Count and Turn	138
10. Counting: The Pendulum Game	139
11. Counting: Counting Forward	140
12. Counting: The Piggy Bank Game	142
13. Writing Numbers: Dotted Numbers	143
14. Writing Numbers: Sandbox and Cards	144

Part 5: Music

Introduction To Music	147
Skills To Develop	149
Activities - Overview	149
Equipment	149
Objectives	149
Ideas for Room Arrangement	150
More Activities	150
Music Through Movement	152
1. Sound Walk	152
2. Sounds Inside	153
3. Body Sounds	154
4. Music in the Dance	155
5. Circle Game	156
6. Move on the Beat	157
7. Bell Game	158

	8.	Whisper Game	159
	9.	Walking a Line Game	160
	10.	Weather Music	161

Music Through Singing..162
   Row, Row, Row Your Boat...162
   Are You Sleeping..163
   Bingo...164
   He's Got the Whole World in His Hands...................................165
   Go In and Out the Window..166
   Oh Where, Oh Where Has My Little Dog Gone..........................167
   The More We Get Together..168
   Kum Ba Yah..169
   The Mulberry Bush..170
   Eency, Weency Spider...171
Children's Music Book of the Orchestra Presentation Instructions.......172
   My Music Book of the Orchestra...173
Music Instruments – Listening and Playing Jars.................................187
   1.   Lesson A: Presenting One Jar and Striker..........................187
   2.   Lesson B: The Octave..187
   3.   Lesson C: The Scale..187
   4.   The Scale in Motion..187
   5.   Making Music..188
Reading Music..189
   1.   First Lesson: The Staff...189
   2.   Second Lesson: The Note..189
   3.   Third Lesson: Playing the Sounds.......................................189
   4.   Fourth Lesson: Seeing the Patterns....................................190
   5.   Fifth Lesson: Listening and Review.....................................190
Introduction To Written Music: Building a Scale on a Staff..................191
Matching Game for Naming the Notes of the C Major Scale................193
Making Music with Rhythm Instruments..195
   1.   Something To Hit..195
   2.   Something To Shake...195
   3.   Something To Pluck..195
Music Instruments – Listening and Playing Rhythm Sticks..................196

Part 6: Creative Dramatics

Introduction To Creative Dramatics..199
Skills To Develop..200
Activities – Overview..200

Equipment..200
Objectives...200
Ideas for Room Arrangement..201
More Activities..201
Creative Dramatics...202
    1.   Songs..202
    2.   Poetry...204
    3.   Finger Plays..206
    4.   Paper Puppets..209
    5.   Puppet Exercises...210
    6.   Other Puppet Ideas..211
    7.   Dancing...212
    8.   Games..213
           A. Imitating Animals...213
           B. Balance Beam..214
           C. Beans...215
           D. Dress-up/Imagination Center...........................216
    9.   Stories and Plays...217

Part 7: Language Arts

Introduction To Language Arts..221
Skills To Develop..222
Activities - Overview..222
Equipment..222
Objectives...222
Ideas for Room Arrangement..223
More Activities..223
Language Arts Projects...224
    1.   Making A "Picture File"..224
    2.   Color Chart Activity...225
    3.   Stop and Tell..226
    4.   Listening To Stories...227
    5.   Discussion About Friends...228
    6.   Animals and Their Babies...229
    7.   Group Language Games..230
    8.   Land or Sea..232
    9.   Learning Alphabet Letters...233
    10.   Learning Numbers: 1-10..234
    11.   Shape Boxes...235
    12.   Sandpaper Letters..236

Sample Phonetic Sounds..237
Sample Printed Letters..238

Part 8: Arts and Crafts

Introduction To Arts and Crafts..241
Skills To Develop..242
Activities - Overview..242
Equipment..242
Objectives...242
Ideas for Room Arrangement..243
More Activities..243
Arts and Crafts Projects..244
    1. Paper Collage...244
    2. Nature Collage...245
    3. Seed and Bean Collage...246
    4. Handprint Bird...247
    5. Paper Bag Bird...248
    6. Block Print with Potato...249
    7. Macaroni Necklaces...250
    8. Spring Baskets..251
    9. Headbands...252
    10. Raindrop Design..253
    11. Kite 254
    12. Tree Drawing..255
    13. Foot Butterfly..256
    14. Flying Bird..257
    15. Pebble Pictures..258
    16. Dough Letters...259

Part 9: Physical Activities

Introduction To Physical Activities...263
    Physical Development..263
    Intellectual Development...263
    Social Development..264
    Emotional Development..264
    Personality Development...264
Skills To Develop..266
Activities - Overview..266
Equipment..266

Objectives...266
Ideas for Room Arrangement..267
More Activities..267
More Physical Activities...268
    1. Basic Body Movements – Walking..268
    2. Basic Body Movements – Running..269
    3. Basic Body Movements – Jumping/Hopping............................270
    4. Basic Body Movements – Balancing..271
    5. Obstacle Course...272
    6. Ball Play..273
    7. Bean Bags...274

Part 10: Preschool Activities as <u>Fun</u>draisers

Preschool Activities as <u>Fun</u>draisers...279
    1. Miniature Garden Indoors...280
    2. Growing Fruit Seeds...281
    3. "Egg" Container Garden...282
    4. Plant a Large Garden...283
    5. Soft Drink Stand..284
    6. Weaving Placemats..285
    7. Peg-Hand-Loom Hand Weaving..286
    8. Recipes for Classroom Fun and <u>Fun</u>draising.........................291
    9. Make Your Own Rock Candy...294
   10. Music and Drama Programs..295
   11. Sock Puppets...296
   12. Finger Puppets...297

Part 11: Preschool "Area" and "Floor Plan" Ideas

City Area Floor Plan "A"..301
City Area Floor Plan "B"..303
City Area Floor Plan "C"..305
Village Preschool Area...307
City or Village Preschool Area..309

Readings List

Readings List..311

Developmental Unit

Teacher - "Preparation"
Enviornment - "Development"
Children - "Ages and Stages"

Developmental Unit

We're preparing the Teachers
    So that they can guide
        Little children
            Through their ages and stages
                That hide the True Wonders
                    Of things deep inside
                        Of the awesome machine
                            Called a child;

For there's more
    Than just physical parts
        To this one
            Who's entrusted to our tender care, ...,
                There's a Mind
                    And a Soul
                        That we must
                            Turn out WHOLE; ...,

                We must learn,
                    So that child
                        Won't be wild!!!

Vanessa Conaway Pace

The Absorbent Mind

The question of how the infant learns language is of great interest to psychologists and teachers, because careful study and observation of this early development can give insight into the development of the mind of the child. And without understanding, how can we teach? We should not attempt to operate on the body without knowledge of anatomy and physiology. So, why should we think that something similar should be done to the mind?

Children belong to social groups and learn gradually, in a *natural* way, from the adults with whom they come in contact. Natural development and adult guidance are of major importance in a child's life. We as teachers and caregivers assume a great responsibility in guiding young children through their early years. We must try to understand and work with the realization of how the mind of a young child learns and develops. Those who care for young children should take the opportunity, if possible, to observe the *spontaneous* manifestation of the infant's growth and development *before these are modified by adult training.*

When we study the baby's development, it becomes obvious that the baby has a very active mind. He may not have the *knowledge* of an adult, but the young child does have an amazing capacity to process his environment. However, he does not learn by waiting passively for instructions from the adult. This is illustrated very clearly by the fact that the child learns to *speak* in the first two years without any direct teaching.

It is interesting to compare this accomplishment with an adult's attempt at learning a foreign language. For most adults it is very difficult to learn a new language. It generally takes many years of study, and a period of residence abroad, before we can express ourselves correctly and understand the language when spoken by the people of the country. Even then, our knowledge will be far from perfect. Every time we open our mouths we will probably show that we are foreigners. In fact, few people ever succeed in speaking a foreign language perfectly, even if they live abroad for many years and speak nothing else. The grammar rules are very complicated. There are many words that differ in slight shades of meaning. Our ear cannot distinguish, nor can our tongue reproduce, the exact pronunciation and intonation. Yet the child learns all this without any teacher in the first few years of life! It does not matter how difficult the

The Absorbent Mind (Continued)

language may be, if it is spoken correctly by the adults who care for the child, he too will learn to speak it perfectly. *And the child starts from nothing!* He is not familiar with words and their use; all this has to be *discovered*. Isn't this a marvelous intellectual achievement? It is amazing! And yet, because it is such a familiar fact, it is generally ignored and forgotten.

Certainly this reveals the child's great intelligence at work. But, this intelligence is functioning in a way that is different from the conscious mental efforts of the adult. In order to emphasize the difference between the learning process of the infant, and that of the adult, let's compare the young child's process to portrait photography, and the adult's to portrait painting. A portrait painter must use a great deal of skill, care, time, and trouble. If the painter wishes to show more that one person on the canvas, or a more detailed background, the work will take longer to finish. However, a photograph can be taken instantaneously, without any work at all. It doesn't matter how many people are standing before the camera, or what kind of background there is, when the shutter moves, everything is recorded in detail. The record is impersonal and accurate, whereas the painting will never be absolutely true to life. It will always show something of the personality of the artist, as well as the subject. People can watch the artist at work, and see how the picture gradually develops into a likeness, but people do not see the photograph being made.

The mind of the adult is like the painter. It is a mind that elaborates with conscious effort, that works and struggles by slow degrees to achieve perfection, but the mind of the child is like the camera. He observes everything, and the record is fixed forever. We speak of this as the *"absorbent mind"* <u>because it can learn so much without effort or fatigue</u>. It masters a modern language in all its complexities. It can even master two languages simultaneously. Such an achievement is quite beyond the powers of the adult. Therefore, to us it seems incredible. But the fact remains that, before the child develops the powers of logic and reason, with which we are familiar, the mind functions in a mysterious way, which we are only beginning to understand. *It is a mistake to disregard and ignore this power just because it is incomprehensible.* This leads to mistakes that make development more difficult and raises barriers to understanding.

Educators must study and observe the baby. They may not discover *how* the unconscious accomplishes its marvelous achievements, but they will begin to

The Absorbent Mind (Continued)

appreciate that it *does*. They will see that the adult must *help*, and not hinder, this development.

In order to learn his mother tongue properly the child needs to hear it spoken constantly. The more he hears it spoken, the better. A Mother, or other caregiver, will give the baby a splendid start in life if she keeps the child with her, instead of leaving him alone. The baby should have a chance to hear adults speaking. To the child, the sound of human speech is like music; it fascinates him. While he can listen he is happy and content. Speech is the most distinctive attribute of mankind. Every human race has a language. Speech is the basis of both our social life, and of our civilization.

Language is an elaborate construction of the intellect, and the fact that *language is actually mastered by the unconscious mind of the infant* should be of the greatest interest. The question at once suggests itself as to <u>what other things may be learned in this way</u>.

Today there are children who develop a precocious mastery of written language and intellectual concepts. Some have *total recall* of everything they read. Some infant prodigies become accomplished mathematicians or musicians at a very early age. All these are cases where the mind *absorbs* the culture from the environment without the slow laborious study of the conscious mind. Since a few children show these remarkable powers, most children must have some capacity to *absorb* words, numbers, and music from the environment. The teacher or caregiver can help by observing the child, answering his questions, and offering exposures to interesting activities, environments, and projects. Perhaps early impressions are as important in the development of intelligence and artistic abilities as they are in the formation of character and personality.

<u>Three Review Points:</u>

1. Remember, young children between the ages of Birth and Six Years learn differently than adults. This process of learning in the young child is called the "Absorbent Mind";
2. Remember, young children learn through movement, repetition, and their five senses (sight, smell, hearing, tasting, and touching). Their environment should be set up to provide activities and experiences that make this way of learning available to the children;

The Absorbent Mind (Continued)

1. Remember, young children have intellectual periods where certain abilities may be learned more naturally and easily than at other times. These readiness periods are called *"sensitive periods"*. A prime example of a *readiness-sensitive period* is the young child's ability to learn language. It appears that young children who are exposed to music, art, math, language, science, and good physical *activities at their readiness-sensitive periods* learn these skills and abilities more easily and naturally.

    ✎   <u>Teacher's Notes:</u> Discussion on The Absorbent Mind:

Teachers/Caregivers

Inner Preparation

As we prepare ourselves for the next school year, there are endless things to catch up with – putting labels on children's books and cubbies, cleaning and arranging the classroom, preparing the materials, and on and on. Sometimes we get so caught up with setting up the physical classroom environment that we lose touch with the need to prepare ourselves inwardly.

The Teacher/Caregiver is truly the most important part of the prepared environment.

Nothing else has a greater influence on the children. The character of the teacher/caregiver will deeply affect the children's inner development and how they relate to life and learning. Since the teacher is the most important part of the children's school environment, the inner preparation of the teacher is essential for the well-being of the children.

We live in a time when stress seems to permeate every aspect of our lives. Not only are the teachers under a lot of pressure and stress, so are the children. We have a great challenge to maintain a stress free atmosphere within ourselves so that the children we work with won't be negatively affected. They must be free to enjoy life's natural energy in a way that is not dissipated by dealing with unnecessary turmoil.

Children try to make sense of their teachers, on whom they are so dependent. A lot of the children's energy can be dissipated in trying to deal with a moody teacher! Can we enter the classroom free from the turmoil of the past and be in the present with the children? Can we maintain in the classroom an atmosphere of happiness and deep involvement? How can we make this school year a year full of growth and free from stress for us and for the children? The trials and turmoil are there, but how we deal with them ultimately will decide how well we deal with stress.

The inward preparation of the teacher is the most crucial preparation of all. It is something we often take for granted and don't think about, but the more conscious we become of it, the more we will see the need for thoroughly preparing ourselves inwardly.

Teachers/Caregivers

Inner Preparation (Continued)

A teacher/caregiver must prepare internally by systematically studying himself so that he can tear out his most deeply rooted defects; those, in fact, which impede his relations with children. This inner preparation needs to be done, not at the beginning of the school year, but continuously during each school day, and throughout our lives.

So, how do you prepare yourself inwardly? First of all, watch your thoughts and motives, and find out about your relationships with others at school. Watch how you affect the children. Your relationships reveal yourself. Look at yourself like an open book, and learn and grow.

In order to discover these subconscious failings, we have need of a special kind of instruction. Here are a few suggestions that may be helpful:

1. Be honest with yourself. Communicate to others with care and integrity.
2. Spend time each day taking care of your inner self. Make time to reflect on each day, even if just for a few minutes!
3. Enter the classroom without emotional baggage. Leave personal issues outside the classroom door. Change hats and say, "I am responsible for the well-being of all these children; my personal problems will not affect the activities of the classroom."
4. Work together. It is very hard not to make distinctions such as, "my class". Focusing on the whole school will bring much greater harmony.
5. Before entering the classroom take a deep breath and exhale all the negativity out of you, pray, breathe in God's energy, and enter the classroom re-vitalized. This simple practice can do a lot for you.
6. Tape record dialogues in the classroom. You will be amazed at what you discover about yourself, and about the children. You will gain special insights into the dynamics of relationships within your room.
7. When making decisions at school, make sure that whatever you decide is in the best interest of the children, and does not arise from personal needs or beliefs.

Teachers/Caregivers

Inner Preparation (Continued)

8. Learn to stay calm with the children, parents, and teaching staff, even in difficult situations. The relationships the children observe among the adults in their lives can have powerful effects on them.
9. Resolve conflicts with the person concerned. If that is not possible, try to work it out with as few people as possible.
10. Be non-competitive. We try to foster non-competition with children, but so often we see competition among staff members. The central focus of our work is the well-being of the children, not self-aggrandizement. There is no point in wasting energy competing with fellow teachers. We are all there for the children. Let's be the best that we can be for them.
11. Be aware of the importance of maintaining a sharing and caring feeling among all that are involved with the school.

Here comes another year, and another opportunity to leave our imprint on the great fragile minds of these children. It is important that we nurture those minds and bring out the best in each child. We must give each child an opportunity to succeed and grow in the best environment we can provide.

What is the goal of education? Is it just imparting academics to children? Or, is there something more? Don't we have an urgent need to go beyond the basics, and prepare the children for life?

Exploring these questions is an important part of the inner preparation of the teacher/caregiver.

It is time to set the tone for the whole year.

These suggestions are not just for the beginning of the school year. They should be utilized routinely. The influence of each teacher/caregiver on each child is really the most important thing in the life of a child, inside and outside the school setting.

Teachers/Caregivers Guidance Suggestions

Techniques of Handling Little Children:

Technique Number 1: Making Contact

1. When talking to or supervising a little child, stoop down, or sit on a low chair, so as to bring your face on a level with his.
2. Rather than calling a child from one side of the room to the other side, walk up to the child, look at him at eye level and talk to him.
3. Use a low quiet voice that helps the child to feel confident and reassured. A soft voice often succeeds in capturing a child's attention when a loud voice will not.
4. Do not hurry the child. The little child's tempo is much slower than ours is. Give the child time to obey, or to respond, or to cooperate. A child needs time to perform and to change his activity. Small children become confused when hurried.
5. Try to be relaxed, confident, and consistent. Do not tell a child one thing one day, and another thing the next day. When limits are necessary, they should be clearly defined and consistently maintained.
6. Answer questions and talk to children, when the occasion calls for it; but avoid talking to them all the time.

Technique Number 2: Giving Directions and Setting Limits

1. Give directions clearly and simply. Have clearly in mind just what you intend to accomplish. Do not give too many suggestions at once; a young child does not have control over his memory. Adults should expect to need to repeat their directions.
2. Before giving a direction, gain the child's attention. Do not interrupt the child's play unnecessarily. When it is necessary to give a command, have an inward conviction in yourself that he will obey; give him time to prepare; and take obedience for granted.
3. Try not to make demands in anger. If you realize that you have done so, explain and apologize to the child.
4. Use the child's name when you talk to him.

Teachers/Caregivers
Guidance Suggestions (Continued)

5. Use language that the child can understand. Help the child to learn the meanings of words by example. For instance: Ringing the bell makes little sense if the child does not understand what it means.
6. Make a clear distinction between requests in which the child has a *choice* of action, and commands that must be followed. Give the child a choice only when you intend to leave the situation up to him. Rather than asking, "Do you want this apron on?", and giving him a chance to refuse, say, "We wear aprons when we paint". Instead of asking, "Do you want to go home?", say, "It is time to go home now". Remember that if you give a child a choice, you are stuck with his decision. In cases where there is a choice involved, show this by your tone. Request, "Would you like to help set tables today?" In matters of routine you might give choice of method. For example: Nap time. You might say, "Can you go to bed by yourself?" (pause), "Or shall I help you?"
7. Try to state things positively, avoiding the negative. Telling a child what to do, rather than what *not* to do is less likely to rouse resistance. Instead of, "Don't stand on the table," say, "We keep our feet on the ground". Or, instead of, "Don't yell in the house," say, "We save our screaming voices for outside". Or, replace, "Don't slam the door", with, "Doors close quietly".
8. Do not use treats or bribes as a means of gaining obedience.
9. Do not make misbehavior exciting; it will only encourage the unwanted behavior, instead of getting rid of it.
10. Teach children not to hit, or to let others hit them. Preventing is better than punishing after an act has happened. If a child hits, explain that it hurts. Tell him you cannot allow him to hurt anyone. Let him know that it is all right to be angry, and to let someone else know that you are angry, but *clearly* state the fact that he cannot hit others.
11. Be reasonable and fair with your directions, and see that they are carried out properly.

Teachers/Caregivers

Guidance Suggestions (Continued)

Technique Number 3: Helping a Child Keep His Self-confidence

1. Look for what is *right* with the child, instead of looking for problems. Praise the type of behavior you want. Continued success is the best reinforcement possible.
2. Be patient. Children need time to develop and improve gradually.
3. Never attempt to change behavior by using words that may make the child feel less respect for himself, such as by *shaming* or *blaming* him, or by making him feel *guilty*. Physical discipline in the classroom is also unacceptable.
4. Never try to motivate a child by making comparisons between one child and another, or by encouraging competition.
5. Show no favoritism.
6. Avoid talking about a child in his presence. If you need to discuss a problem, do it when the child is not present.
7. If a child has a toilet accident, quietly take the child aside and help him change his clothes without commenting on the accident. Give the child support and warmth.
8. If a child gets hurt, comment, "That hurt, didn't it?" Provide comfort. If the injury is minor, casually redirect the child to another activity, going with him if he needs adult help and guidance. A bandage may be offered as a "quick healer" to reassure the child he is all right. If the injury is serious, take appropriate first aid precaution, and call the parent, if necessary.

Technique Number 4: When To Step In

1. Forestalling is a most effective way of handling problems. Learn to foresee and prevent, rather than mop-up after a difficulty. If the situation is not dangerous, give the children a chance to work out their own problems before stepping in. Step into a social conflict situation only when necessary to prevent injury, or to suggest a socially approved solution to a difficulty. Children need to learn self-reliance as well as cooperation.
2. When children are working or playing well, do not interfere – only observe.

Teachers/Caregivers

Guidance Suggestions (Continued)

3. Allow the child to learn by experiment. Help him only when it is necessary. Give the opportunity for trial and error, and trial and success. This will help him to develop independence. You, and the child, will be pleased when, as he zips his coat he says, "I did it all by myself".
4. Gradually withdraw your physical and verbal help as the child progresses toward independence.
5. Some occasions that call for adult help:

   A. When child is:
   - Over-excited and uncontrolled;
   - Aimless in activity – flitting from one thing to another;
   - Under tension or strain;
   - Restless, fatigued or sleepy;
   - Uncertain as to what to do;
   - In danger.

   B. When a child has:
   - Tried a long time and seems about to fail;
   - Such a big job to do that he doesn't even want to start trying;
   - Made a mistake, and cannot resolve it himself;
   - A new situation to meet, if he cannot adjust by himself;
   - Difficulty in handling materials or equipment;
   - Been distracted from his undertaking.

   C. When a child doesn't know how;
   D. When he asks for help;
   E. When he seems fearful and lacking in confidence;
   F. When his skill is uncertain or limited;
   G. When a child begins, but gives up easily.

Teachers/Caregivers

Guidance Suggestions (Continued)

Technique Number 5: Listen and Love

1. Listen to children. You will learn many valuable things. When a child has something to say:
   - Listen all the way through;
   - Express interest;
   - Avoid correcting the child's use of language. Merely use the words properly so that he will learn from your good example. Correcting a child may hinder the flow of words.
   - If you cannot understand the child's mumbling, repeat a few key words that you do understand so that he knows you are interested.
   - If a child asks for something, and you cannot tell what he is saying, say, "I do not understand what you are telling me. Show me what you want and I will get it." Then follow his lead.
2. Love and accept each child as he is. Remember that each child is different. Let each child grow and proceed at his own rate.
3. Let the children know you like them by making physical contact with them, or by simply saying, "I like you!"
4. Set up clear Discipline Policies in the Center that show respect toward the child, and are helpful for the teacher/caregiver.

Environment

A Classroom Planned For Learning

<u>Children Need To:</u>
- Use their changing bodies;
- Explore the world around them;
- Grow in language
- Learn to work with others;
- Think of themselves as capable people.

<u>Children Learn By:</u>
- Testing and exercising their bodies;
- Handling, tasting, smelling, hearing, seeing;
- Hearing language about their own experiences;
- Acting out things, living things over;
- Sharing materials and people;
- Being accepted;
- Solving problems in their own way

A well-planned classroom helps the child to develop and invites him to learn. A classroom for young children is planned with Learning Centers, which allow the child to learn, by doing. The child grows in confidence and self-respect as he learns to work with others, and to meet and solve problems.

A well-planned classroom prevents many discipline problems, and allows the teacher to know the children as individuals:

1. The child is able to choose from any activities, and move from one activity to another as he wishes. We want the child to learn in ways that are natural to him.
2. The daily schedule gives one large block of time, about an hour, to activities in the Learning Centers. We want the child to have many first-hand experiences;
3. Equipment and supplies are placed where the child can reach and return them without adult help. We want the child to become independent. (See "How To Start A Classroom" sheet in this section.)
4. Supplies are organized and returned to their proper places after being used. We want the child to know order. (See "How To Start A Classroom" sheet in this section.)

Environment

How To Start A Classroom

In the beginning you do not let the children loose in the classroom to pick and choose activities. You also do not fill all your tables with games and let the children loose to play.

1. Freedom must be earned; you work toward it. Initially the teacher must be the dominant person, and gradually she can become less and less so;
2. The classroom must be prepared *before* the children come in;...chairs around the tables, shelves in order, projects ready for group art and concept times;
3. In Circle Time/Gathering Time ask the children their names. Spend time making them feel comfortable. Tell stories, sing songs, give some games involved around the concept of what "quiet" means, and what it means to "move slowly and carefully";
4. Talk about the classroom. Introduce the children to where things are located on the shelves, and how to handle the things. Talk about the different Learning Centers. Make clear how many children are allowed in a Center at one time. Roll play how the children should handle themselves in these Centers;
5. Give the children such things as clay, coloring, water coloring, and simple toys to play with the first few days of orientation;
6. In the meantime, as a group, show the children how to take materials from the shelves, play with them, and return them to the shelves;
7. Gradually put out the new materials on the shelf. Present each one to the group, as suggested in Number 6, before placing it on the shelf;
8. Soon the whole class is able to participate in group learning, where the teacher is the dominant person, and in individual learning, where the children are able to choose what they want to work with, and whom they want to play with. In this individual learning situation the teacher circulates and gently "directs" and "encourages" the children, rather than dominating the scene;
9. Group learning and individual learning provide a classroom where the child can grow more fully at his or her own pace. It also provides the teacher with the chance to give each one of the children in his or her care what they may need in the way of attention, special one-to-one opportunities for growth, and the love they all deserve.

Children

Ages and Stages

Birth To One Year

Infants grow at a very fast rate. By the end of the first year they will have tripled in their birth weight, if proper nutrition, exercise, and sleep are available daily. Infant care requires a warm, responsive, dependable adult caregiver. A lot of holding, cuddling, and loving attention will result in a warm relationship between the baby and its caregiver.

Some record keeping should occur when caring for infants. Things such as eating, sleeping, bowel movements, and activities should be recorded. Also, a growth chart is helpful, which would include weight and length of the baby or infant.

Right from birth the infant starts to learn. Within the infant the mental powers of the adult are being constructed: Reason, consciousness, and memory. These, plus additional powers of muscular coordination, orientation in space, and the power of speech are being learned. Your infant is not at all passive! He achieves knowledge of what is happening around him through what he experiences. He does not just receive sensations passively and react mechanically. He discriminates and concentrates according to his inner impressions. His behavior is influenced by previous experiences. Behavioral patterns are established and eventually the powers of the adult mind are built up. We cannot fully understand this process, but it is important as caregivers to know the process is occurring in our infants. We should be diligent in providing the necessary care that will aid this growth.

If we wish to help the baby in his or her development we must be observant, ready to provide what is needed, rather than anxious to enforce a rigid routine. If he sleeps all morning, that is good. But if he wakes and does not go to sleep again, but frets and cries, that is different. It may be a sign of growth and development. The caregiver need not feel anxious and worried that something will go wrong if the baby does not get his sleep. The baby will sleep when he is tired. But his sleep is not the only thing he needs. His arms and legs will not grow strong through just sleep – they must have exercise as well; and, if the body needs exercise, the mind needs experience. The baby must

Children

Ages and Stages

Birth To One Year (Continued)

begin to explore his environment through his senses. The caregiver must put him in a cradle or basket where she is working so he can see what is going on.

The young baby cannot see very well at first, but he will be happy if he can hear his caregiver moving, talking, and singing to him. He will lie there, learning to focus and move his eyes, to control his hands and legs, and to make wonderful babbling sounds with his mouth. None of this development will go well without the stimulus of human companionship. The first thing the baby learns to recognize is the face of someone smiling and talking to him. He will greet this with smiles and coos of delight. Later on, when he gains sufficient control of his muscles to hold his head steady, he may be supported with pillows so he can have a good view of the room.

Now, besides giving the child the opportunity to observe the environment to patiently understand and interpret his needs, we can also help by keeping to a regular routine, and having everything arranged in a consistent order. In the bewildering multiplicity of impressions that the child must learn to recognize and classify, the familiar objects of the environment, such as furniture, become "landmarks" on which he depends.

We know the baby begins to become familiar with his environment and routine because babies soon begin to recognize that preparations are being made for feeding. This can be seen because they will show patience, or anticipation, quite clearly. In the same way, a baby begins to know when it is time for him to be bathed or taken outside. To help this process the child should never be snatched up and hurried away. We should speak to him first and explain what we are doing – giving him time to realize what is happening. It is wrong to assume that he cannot understand. At first he does not, but very soon he will. The loving voice that speaks to him awakens his interest and attention, and understanding comes. In this way the baby's education begins.

Children

Ages and Stages

Birth To One Year (Continued)

<u>Caregiver Guidelines:</u>

1. Respond to the Infant's cries. This develops their sense of trust and security;
2. Hold and cuddle Infants when feeding them. This is very important in the development of their self-worth and sense of security;
3. Infants should be placed in new places and new positions so they can see you and each other;
4. Respect an Infant's natural schedule. Most all babies have a regular routine for eating, sleeping, and soiling their diapers. If you are caring for many Infants try to be as regular in these matters as possible, and remember to keep a record of this care;
5. Infants like a variety of objects to look at, especially bright, colored, moving objects;
6. The environment should be rich, with pleasant sounds – music, soft voices, etc.;
7. Infants love to feel, touch, smell, and taste. They learn through their senses. Provide simple experiences in these areas;
8. Help Infants to develop their movements. Wiggling, kicking in the air, rolling over, following you with their eyes, gradually sitting up, raising arms and legs in the air are a few movements. By twelve months eating finger foods, drinking from a cup, crawling, pulling themselves to a standing position, and opening and closing cupboard doors can be added to the movement list. Give Infants freedom to move around.
9. Talk to Infants and read to Infants. With time they will understand that words have meaning and can be used to identify objects;
10. Infants like to play simple little games, like peek-a-boo, where you hide your face in your hands and then peek out at them. Holding the Infant while spending time with simple reading, finger plays, and conversations is a great way to develop their love for their caregivers and security with their world.

Remember, the caregiver is the most important thing in a child's life!

Children

Ages and Stages

One Year To Two Years

By one the Infant is starting to develop a real personality. Growth continues to be rapid. First steps and first words are wonderful events.

At around one-and-a-half (18 months or so) Toddlers begin to walk, run, and climb. A sense of independence begins to develop. "Imitating" everything, and "pretending" are favorite activities. Remember "inner growth" of reasoning, and memory is occurring. Toddlers are very aware of what is going on around them through what they experience. Along with "inner growth", outward growth is also developing. Again, caregivers should try to provide activities that aid in these developmental areas.

<u>Caregiver Guidelines:</u>

1. Play with your Toddlers. Enjoy some "play time" rolling a ball, encouraging movement, relaxing and having fun dancing to music. Encourage the Toddlers to wiggle, sway, and bounce;
2. Look at simple books with your Toddlers. Point to animals, objects, and people pictures, naming them. Encourage them to name the objects and talk about the pictures. Read short stories every day;
3. Teaching Toddlers simple "finger plays", songs, and simple dances are fun activities;
4. Provide simple toys for your Toddlers to play with. Things that are fun to pull, poke, and squeeze are delightful. Soft stuffed animals are enjoyable;
5. Talk frequently to Toddlers to increase language skills. During dressing time clothes or body parts can be named. For example: "See this blue shirt? Put your arms into the sleeves." When the Toddler is eating, identify the food. When taking a walk, point out the trees, water, grass, and sky. Naming things in the Toddler's everyday world helps language development, and is a fun activity for them.
6. Games of running, climbing, and walking are very important. These "Large Motor Skills" strengthen Toddlers in their rapidly developing bodies. Games for developing "Small Motor Skills"

Children

Ages and Stages

One Year To Two Years (Continued)

should also be made available. For example: Let the Toddlers drop clothespins into a plastic bottle, or provide containers with loose-fitting lids, and encourage the Toddlers to open and close them.

Remember, the caregiver is the most important thing in a child's life!

✎ <u>Teacher's Notes:</u> Birth To Two Years:

Children

Ages and Stages

Two Years To Three Years

"Independent" is the word to characterize two-year-olds. These Toddlers are discovering the world. They can walk, and therefore the world is theirs! Emotions are very changeable from laughter to anger in a given moment. They spend a lot of time pushing, pulling, exploring, and touching.

Because Toddlers are gaining more and more independence does not mean they do not remain very attached to their teachers/caregivers. They will explore their surroundings, but still remain very close to their caregivers for support and trust. Socially they are interested in other children, but must be shown how to play with others. Toddlers require caregivers with much patience and energy. Flexibility, vigilance, and nurturing are also very helpful!

<u>Teacher/Caregiver Guidelines:</u>

1. Many of the ideas used for Toddlers ages one to two can be used with older Toddlers ages two to three. (See "One Year To Two Years" sheet in this section.);
2. Older Toddlers are more active and skillful at opening doors and getting into mischief! Make sure their area is "*safe*" to play in;
3. Toddlers love to help with simple chores. Let them help you pick up toys, put on their clothes and eat independently,...(as is possible!);
4. Language building skills should be one of the teacher/caregiver's main goals with Toddlers. Read aloud to them. Encourage them to look at books with large pictures...alone, or with you. Expand the Toddlers knowledge of words. Speak in short sentence to them. For example, if he or she says "more," and points to the milk, say, "Elizabeth wants more milk. Here is your milk, Elizabeth." Add new information to what a child is saying. For example: "Yes, that's a soft stuffed animal you are playing with, Isaac";
5. Give older Toddlers choices: "Do you want to drink juice or milk?" "Do you want to wear the blue or red shirt?" ....;
6. At this stage Toddlers are focusing on how to handle themselves physically. Do not expect them to share or take turns. Learning to

Children

Ages and Stages

Two Years To Three Years (Continued)

share can be gently shown them. Gradually they will grow into it – and learn;

7. Provide music for your Toddlers. Play "parade" and do little dances with them. Sing and do finger plays. They love it!
8. Water play, sand, sifting, pouring, stirring, and clay are a few fun activities;
9. Ride-on toys, pulling and pushing toys, cardboard boxes to crawl into, and drawing pictures are a few appropriate activities.

Remember, Toddlers become very attached to their teacher/caregiver. Your love, calmness, soothing voice, and patience are of prime importance to their little lives. You are the most important thing in a child's life.

✐ <u>Teacher's Notes:</u> Two Years To Three Years:

Children

Ages and Stages

Three-Year-Olds

A three-year-old spends a lot of time exploring his or her world. Watching and observing are favorite activities. Imitating what is seen is very common. Repetition is learning at this age. (Actually, repetition is learning for children ages birth-through-6.) Repeating activities, doing and undoing puzzles, for example, satisfies this type of growth. These sequences are important to future understandings of change and consistency.

<u>Fun</u>

Three-year-olds love Large Motor Activities such as climbing, running, and jumping. Physical Activities inside the Preschool and outside in the yard should be provided regularly.

Although sharing is not something a three-year-old does naturally, training needs to begin now in order for it to become a natural part of a child's life.

<u>Teacher/Caregiver Guidelines:</u>

1. Because many children may not have been completely toilet trained by the age of three, accidents may happen. The teacher/caregiver should be patient, and avoid shaming a child in such a circumstance. Using words of encouragement, quietly take the child aside and help them change their clothes;
2. Encourage Fine Motor Skills involving hand-eye coordination by providing "hands-on" shelf games for the children. Many of these activities are listed in this *Guidebook*;
3. Large and Small Motor Activities are very important at this age. Creative Dramatics can be a fun way of incorporating these activities. Running like a deer, hopping like a rabbit, waddling like a duck are examples. The *Guidebook* section on "Physical Activities" and "Creative Dramatics" will be very helpful in these areas. Music is also vital and fun! (See *Guidebook*.);

Children

Ages and Stages

Three-Year-Olds (Continued)

4. Language is another important area. Talk frequently with the children. Use short sentences, ask questions, and remember to *listen* to their responses. Read books to the children, and re-read the same book if they want to hear it. Remember, <u>repetition is learning</u> at this age. Have the children repeat the story and discuss ideas and events. Read poetry, sing songs, and talk with "puppets" (See *Guidebook*.);
5. Involve the children in exploring objects, patterning objects, counting objects (this can be done with simple math games), cooking projects, science ideas. (Again, see your *Guidebook*.);
6. Provide the children with simple art projects. Hands-on activities delight them, and are essential to their growth;
7. Every Preschool should have a "Home Center" area where the children can pretend and do very simple household tasks. It is natural for children at this age to imitate adults.

Remember, the teacher/caregiver is the most important thing in a child's life!

✐ <u>Teacher's Notes:</u> Three-Year-Olds:

Children

Ages and Stages

Four-Year-Olds

Life is exciting for a four-year-old. They are very active, adventurous, bold, often impatient, and a lot of the time can be silly and eager for fun. Their imagination is very much "alive", causing them to go from reality to "make believe" easily. Exaggerations are common.

Four-year-olds love to do things, and feel good about what they can do. They like to try new things, and generally show confidence.

A lot of physical activity should be provided for four-year-olds. Running, jumping, walking, and climbing games and free play are a few fun activities.

The practice in sharing that they have done in the earlier years has prepared the four-year-old for new opportunities for making friends, sharing activities, and enjoying other social activities.

Four-year-olds need to feel important. Praise and encouragement are vital.

<u>Teacher/Caregiver Guidelines:</u>

1. Art activities are enjoyed by four-year-olds. Play dough, collages made from magazine pictures, fabrics, and newsprint, coloring, and painting are just a few ideas (See *Guidebook*.);
2. Large Motor Activities outside and Small Motor Activities in the classroom are vital. Preschoolers learn through moving, touching, seeing, hearing, and smelling (the five senses), so Preschool "shelf games" are essential to their learning. Many ideas are presented in the *Guidebook* – puzzles, pouring games, coloring, and clay, to mention a few;
3. Creative Dramatics, stories, puppets, music, dancing, singing, and drama are just a few enjoyable ways for the four-year-old to experience the freedom and independence he or she should have;

Children

Ages and Stages

Four-Year-Olds (Continued)

4. Language is also important. Read aloud each day. Stories, poetry, magazine articles on science or geography are a few ideas. Have the children learn songs, rhymes, and finger plays. Speak in sentences to the children, and encourage them to speak in sentences. Listen to them;
5. Encourage the children in writing and words. Expose them to printed letters and numbers;
6. Help the children to start enjoying numbers – rote counting, finger counting, sight counting, group counting, as well as math (See *Guidebook*.);
7. Science is another area of learning. Nature walks, as well as science projects, should be in the Preschool classroom (See *Guidebook*.).

It is important that teachers/caregivers enjoy a sense of adventure with their four-year-old. Limits must be set, and limits must be consistent and reasonable. Within these limits the teacher/caregiver and four-year-old should enjoy each other.

Remember, the teacher/caregiver is the most important thing in a child's life!

✎ <u>Teacher's Notes:</u> Four-Year-Olds:

Children

Ages and Stages

Five-Year-Olds

One of the most wonderful characteristics of a five-year-old is their love for life. At five years their coordination skills and intellectual capabilities prompt a certain self-confidence.

Five-year-olds love to share ideas and experiences in small groups. Even though sharing in general (toys and turns) comes a little easier as the child gains experience, some direction may still be necessary from the teacher/caregiver if the child is having difficulty sharing.

The Preschool program for five-year-olds should be challenging and full of opportunities to explore new things, such as Arts, Crafts, Music, Science, Math, Language, and Physical Activities. (See *Guidebook* for ideas and projects.)

Teachers/Caregivers should know that all children love genuine praise and encouragement. The five-year-old especially loves praise, and responds to the teacher/caregiver who will listen with a sympathetic heart to his or her needs.

Teacher/Caregiver Guidelines:

1. Five-year-olds assign roles and get ideas from playing with each other. Home Centers, Dramatic Play, Puppets, Blocks, Arts and Crafts, Music, and hands-on games, toys, and activities are all wonderful means of developing their imaginations and small motor skills;
2. By five it is pretty evident whether a child is right or left handed. Let the child determine which hand he or she chooses to use. Coloring, ruler work, printing of letters and numbers, and hands-on shelf activities should be available to aid in the strengthening of hand-eye coordination;
3. Language is a very important area to provide for five-year-olds. Stories should be read daily by the teacher/caregiver. Poetry, Creative Dramatics, Puppets, Music, and Finger Plays are fun ways to increase vocabulary and creativity;

Children

Ages and Stages

Five-Year-Olds (Continued)

4. Math and Science are two other interesting and important parts of a preschooler's day (See *Guidebook*.);
5. Physical Activity should be a regular part of the five-year-old's day. Outside games and free play, as well as inside games, dancing, rhythm, and drama activities help with the fast growing development of the five-year-old.

Use the *Guidebook* for the suggested activities mentioned above.

Remember, the teacher/caregiver is the most important thing in a child's life!

✎ <u>Teacher's Notes:</u> Five-Year-Olds:

www.fortheloveofchildrenbook.com   E-mail: info@.fortheloveofchildrenbook.com

Part 1
Gathering Time

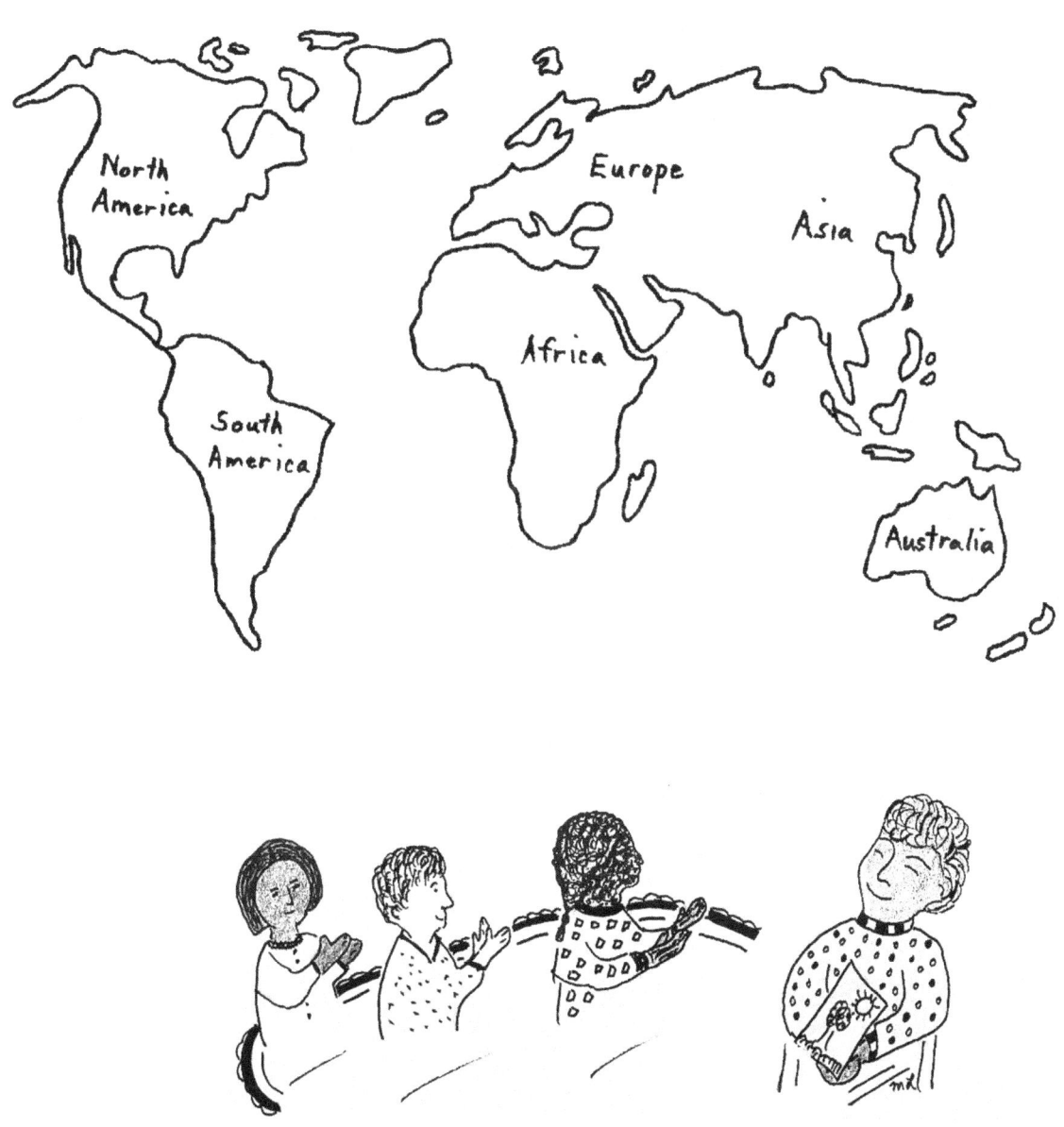

In Gathering Time
    We find other Friends
        Who sing us a Welcome
            And give life
                A new lens

Through which we can look
    At our world
        And each other
            As we plan out our day
            In our world
                Called
                    "DISCOVER"!!!

Vanessa Conaway Pace

Introduction To Gathering Time/Circle Time

Gathering Time should be an essential part of the preschool classroom. Sitting in a circle together on a regular basis brings about a bonding of the Teacher with the children. It enables the Teacher to get acquainted with the children, and the children to get acquainted with their Teacher and each other. The gathering Time should be regular and fun. Warm times of sharing should occur. This is also a good time for instruction in behavior, classroom arrangement and materials.

Gathering Time Expectations

In order to have a successful, controlled Gathering Time the children should be thoroughly shown what is expected of them. Here is one successful approach.

1. Place small mat on the floor in a circle facing the Teacher. Instruct each child to sit on one mat;
2. Show the child how to sit with legs crossed and hands in their laps;
3. Explain that they are to sit quietly and listen to the Teacher, who will tell them what will be happening (Story, Music, Instruction, ...);
4. Tell them that they may share with the group when they raise their hand and the Teacher calls their name.
5. The Teacher should excuse them from the Gathering Time when it is finished (15 to 30 minutes, depending on activity and interest level).

Note: Laying down clear rules provides a security for the child. It gives the child a clear idea of what is expected, and frees up his mind to enter in to whatever activity the Teacher is presenting.

Introduction To Gathering Time/Circle Time (Continued)

Gathering Times - When - Why

<u>Suggestions:</u>

1. First thing in the morning before other activities start:

    ⇨ Welcome children;
    ⇨ Present Calendar - Name of month, day, year;
    ⇨ Weather Chart - Weather of the day, season;
    ⇨ Give any instructions pertinent to the day;
    ⇨ Present any activities, new or review.

2. During the morning and/or afternoon for a Story Time;
3. During the morning and/or afternoon for group Music, Dancing, Creative Dramatics;
4. Whenever a new material is introduced into the classroom it should be introduced during Gathering Time, where the Teacher shows how it is used and handled, and where it will be located in the room;
5. Classroom conduct and center play activities should be introduced. Children should be shown how to handle themselves in the classroom. Role-play should be used - Walking Feet, Quiet Voices, Sharing, etc.

Introduction To Gathering Time/Circle Time (Continued)

I. <u>Presentation of Games and Activities: General Points:</u>

   A. The caregiver must be well acquainted with the game or activity. Clear presentation is important;

   B. The presentation should not be too lengthy. Preschoolers have short attention spans;

   C. The presentation should be interesting and fun in order to stimulate the child's interest;

   D. Repeating the presentation is necessary. Repetition is learning. At this time child participation may occur. The repetition helps the child to feel comfortable doing the activity alone later;

   E. The caregiver should show the children where the game or activity being presented will be located in the classroom. A fun learning game called "Roll Play" can be used at this time. The caregiver during a Gathering Time, after explaining the activity or game, places it on the shelf where it will be available to the children. The children can take turns going to the shelf, taking the game, playing with it, and returning it to the shelf where it belongs. This teaches the child what is expected of him or her when using the game during classroom activity time later.

   The principle is:

   - Picking the game,
   - Using the game, and
   - Returning the game to its proper place.

   Children of this age (3-5) love to be independent and orderly. What better way to start this training?

   F. Do not clutter the classroom. Too many activities and games can be confusing. The classroom should have enough activities for all the children to be busy. The rest of the activities should be stored in boxes and rotated as needed.

Introduction To Gathering Time/Circle Time (Continued)

2. <u>Example of Group Presentation: Handling a Book:</u>

   ☺ <u>Skills:</u>

   - ☺ To help the child gain co-ordination and self-sufficiency in learning how to handle things correctly and comfortably;
   - ☺ Enabling the child to look at books without adult help at home and at school;
   - ☺ To help a child learn a careful way to pick up a book, to carry a book, to open a book, to turn its pages, and to replace a book carefully to the place from which it was taken;
   - ☺ To help prepare the child for Language Activities;
   - ☺ To give a child experience in group learning.

   ✂ <u>Materials To Be Used:</u>

   - ✂ A few (3-6) hard cover books with interesting pictures and illustrations inside (rotate books every week);
   - ✂ A set up area in room where the books will be available for the children when they want to sit quietly and look at them.

   ☞ <u>Goals of Presentation:</u>

   - ☞ Handling the book properly: Taking the book off of the shelf or table, carrying it carefully to the place where it will be enjoyed;
   - ☞ Opening the book and turning the pages gently from the top right-hand corner;
   - ☞ Returning the book to its original space on the shelf or table when finished. Role play the procedure with the children.

   During Gathering Time each area and each piece of equipment and each activity needs to be presented to the children before it is placed in the classroom for the children's use. This is a gradual process. Little by little the classroom grows in activity centers and the corresponding equipment.

   ✎ <u>Teacher's Notes:</u> Discussion on results of activity; open format; Teacher records own results.

Gathering Time
Circle Time

Listening, Learning, Sharing

Skills To Develop	Activities – Overview
• Listening To Instructions	Teacher Instructions; Stories; Directional Skills; How to handle oneself and the equipment in the room
• Language	Stories; Poems; Art; and Music
• Memory	Recalling stories, poems, instructions
• Participation in Group Activities	Dancing; Discussions; Games
• Sharing Ideas	Develop stories, activities - - - Show and Tell – Things or Events
• Listening To Others	Sitting still and listening respectfully to others' ideas and experiences

Equipment:

Calendar; Alphabet Chart; Number Chart; Storybooks; Poems; Singing and Dancing Activities; Pictures of Classroom Conduct Skills

Objectives:

- Group awareness:
  - Bonding between Teacher and children;
  - Cooperating with the group; Working together on group projects;
  - Being considerate toward others; Sharing space and ideas;
  - Taking turns; Waiting while others speak; Listening to others;
  - Getting acquainted with classmates through group games and sharing time.

Ideas for Room Arrangement: Gathering Time – Circle Time:

Floor Area where a circle of children, sitting on the floor, can gather as a group:

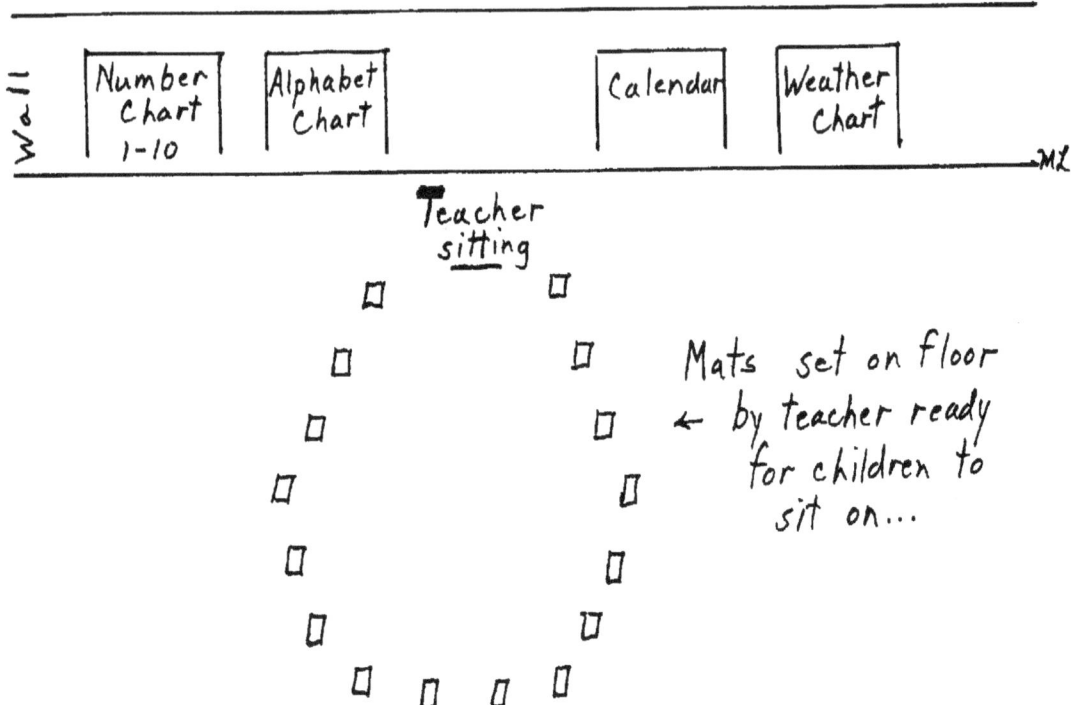

More Activities (See also Unit Activities in Creative Dramatics and Music Sections):

- Room orientation;
- Quiet activities (Bell Game, Whisper Game);
- Group problem-solving (How we live, play, and work together);
- The class could write a story;
- The class could make up a dance.

Concepts – Preschool Level

Size and Contour

Big – little
Tall – short
Thick – thin
Narrow – wide
Round – square
Circles
Curved – straight

Content

Box full
Jarful
Empty – full
Cupful
Handful

Amount

All – some
Many
Whole – part
Each
More – less
Pair
Few – many
One – half
Less than – more than
None

Tactile Sensations

Hot – cold
Warm – cool
Painful
Smooth – rough

Time and Seasons

Early – late
Fast – slow
On time
Night – day
Morning – afternoon
Noon
Day – week
Winter – Summer
Spring – Fall
Clock, hour; o'clock
Late, later, latest
Early, earlier, earliest

Money and Money Terms

(Sample: Introduce *local* currencies and teach the relationships between the basic terms.)
One cent – penny
Nickel – five cents
Dime – 10 cents
Quarter – 25 cents

Comparison

Heavy – light
Faster – slower
Fast, faster, fastest
Taller – shorter
More – most
Tallest – shortest
Higher – lower
Biggest – smallest
Large – small

Location

Up – down
In – out
On – off
Front – back
Beginning – end
Before – after
High – low
Left – right
Under – over
Next
Close – closer
Middle
Above – below
Top – bottom

Number Terms

Add to
In
All together
Subtract
Take away from
Numbers 1 to 5

Ability to count articles or objects up to 10

Ability to subtract with objects up to 5

Ability to do rote counting

www.fortheloveofchildrenbook.com   E-mail: info@.fortheloveofchildrenbook.com

Part 2
Growing Exercises

59

In Growing Exercises
    We learn
        To take care of ourselves
            And give others
                A turn;

As we take care of
    The Earth
        And the people
            Around us
                And develop new skills
                    Using things
                        That surround us.

                                    Vanessa Conaway Pace

Introduction To Growing Exercises

Practical life activities give the child an understanding of his environment and how it works. The child enjoys all types of work. He also enjoys keeping the environment beautiful for all to use. This work builds the child's self-esteem. In addition, practical life activities also develop manual dexterity.

In the school and in the home adults must never complain about their work in front of the child. At a young age the child learns by imitating the adult. If adults dislike work, the child will learn that all types of work are to be avoided. He will apply this to school learning as well as to manual skills. He must have a respect for all types of work well done.

The child must not be conditioned to work only for himself. As a mature adult he will choose the type of work that he is good at, and that he enjoys. In doing this work he will earn a living, but at the same time he will be contributing to the society in which he lives. By working well he will retain his self-esteem and be happy. All types of necessary work, done well, contribute to the good of the whole society. Young people should adopt the kind of work that they enjoy doing. Academic, medical, manual, and most other types of work are creative.

In the home, and in the school, children should be encouraged to put things away in the right place, and to clean up any mess they have inadvertently made while working. In this, the adult sets an example. In the home, or in the school, there must be shelves, etc., supplied at the child's height so that he can do this.

If a child is having a difficult day (and you as a Teacher would know that), or, if a child does not want to put his things away, or, before he understands how to do so, the adult must give generous help. Here are a few suggestions:

- The Teacher/Caregiver can offer to help the child, ("Shall I help you?", or, "If you don't want to, I will do it *this time*".);
- The Teacher/Caregiver can ask other children if they want to help the child, ("Who would help Johnny put his things away?");
- The Teacher/Caregiver can ask other children to help the Teacher/Caregiver ("Would someone like to help me put Johnny's things away?").

We are *not* saying that this is the norm. This is the exception. The *goal* is the *training* of the child, not getting the specific task done. In this way the

Introduction To Growing Exercises (Continued)

children learn to help each other, and the child who is helped will be the first to help others later, and to do the job himself. This type of training should occur at home, and at school. Later, as older children, when their developmental need to do this work is over, they will help willingly and cheerfully, knowing that everyone helps to run the home, which belongs to all the family.

These activities must be taken seriously and taught seriously. The child must be given the dignity of a worker, for he works very hard.

The area of cooking with your preschooler is a good example of how all the "Growing Exercises" help in the development of a young child. Your preschooler is very able to be a real help in the kitchen - setting the table (which aids his concept of sets in preparation for math), washing dishes, (which makes him feel successful and independent), and cooking.

While a completed dish looks like a monumental task to a child, he learns that it is simply a series of steps - most of which he can do. (And, helping cook a meal often inspires a picky eater!) Cooking is more than enjoyment. It is probably the best example of a single learning experience that incorporates many intellectual tasks: Language stimulation, motor skills, development of math concepts, and science.

The Benefits of Preschool Cookery

Science

During the cooking process children explore by tasting the ingredients, smelling the changes as they cook, feeling the ingredients before and after cooking. They begin to understand physical changes through the application of heat and cold, i.e., as raw apples become "mushy" applesauce, as ice melts to water, as water heats to steam, as gelatin which was hot and liquid sets to wiggly solidity. They learn about chemical changes as they add yeast to dough and watch bread rise or soda and vinegar to gingerbread batter.

A child learns there is a consistency to his world and he can control it. If a certain recipe is followed with its specific ingredients, measurements and steps, it will yield the same result. Mixing flour, salt and alum will always make playdough, never cookie batter.

Introduction To Growing Exercises (Continued)

Language Stimulation

Children learn to compare ingredients that look similar, such as sugar and salt, and yet are different.

They learn new words to describe what is happening, such as *dissolving* gelatin powder in hot water, *grating* cheese for tacos, shredding lettuce for salad, bringing the soup to a *boil*, *freezing* the ice cream mixture as they turn the handle on the ice cream maker, *creaming* shortening and sugar for cookies. To further enhance cooking experiences, coordinate your excursions – shopping at the Market, driving to the fields at picking time, visiting dairy farms, harvesting fruits in season, or visiting a bakery. A good rainy day activity would be cutting out magazine pictures of foods that you have cooked together, or plan to cook soon.

They observe and begin to verbalize about texture, consistency, taste and smell, as soft cookie dough bakes to become crisp cookies with definite shape and form. They begin then to understand opposites: Hot and cold, sweet and sour, hard and soft, wet and dry, raw and cooked.

Recipe For A Happy Day

(Especially while doing cooking projects with your children!)

1 Cup friendly words
2 Heaping cups of understanding
4 Heaping tsp. Time and patience
Pinch of warm personality
Dash of humor

Measure words carefully. Add heaping cup of understanding, use generous amounts of time and patience. Cook on the front burner, but keep temperature low. Do not boil. Add generous dash of humor and a pinch of warm personality. Season to taste with spice of life. Serve in individual molds.

Growing Exercises

<u>Skills To Develop</u>

- Care of Person
- Care of Environment
- Plant and Garden Care
- Cooking

<u>Activities – Overview</u>

Dressing; Buttoning; Putting on coat; Grooming; Washing hands etc.;
Dusting Game; Sweeping game
Observe needs of plants; Cultivate garden
Preparing vegetables; Simple cooking

<u>Equipment:</u>

Refer to section entitled "Extended Growing Exercises". Equipment will depend on the unit you are studying.

<u>Objectives:</u>

- Practical care of person;
- Practical care of environment;
- Fine hand-eye coordination;
- Confidence in self;
- Awareness of self, others, and environment through projects and hands-on activities.

Ideas for Room Arrangement: Growing Exercises

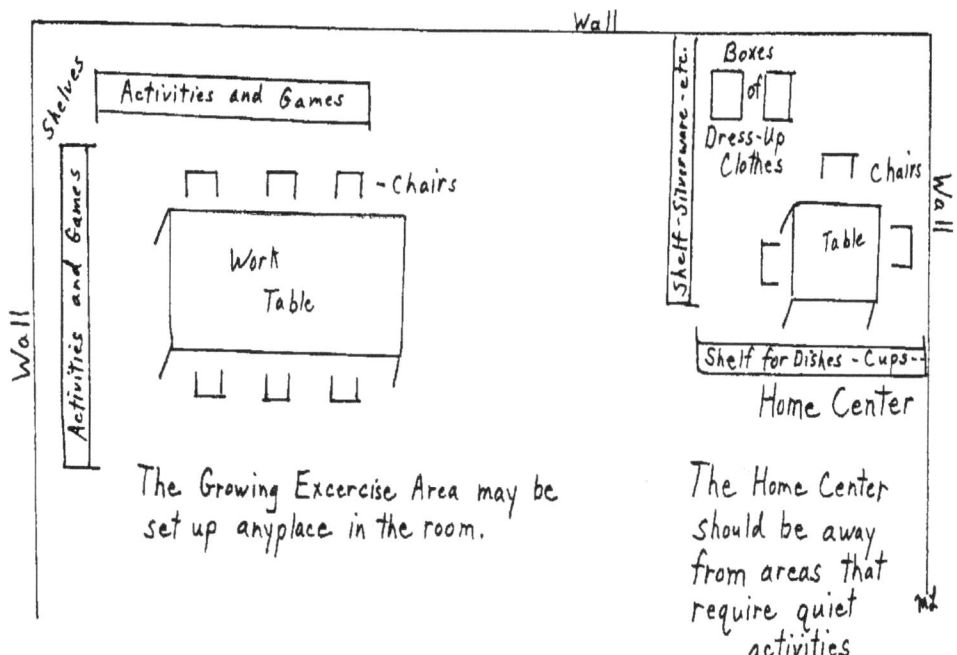

More Activities:

- Stringing Macaroni, Beads – Hand-eye coordination, creating patterns, concept of combining colors;
- Sorting things, like different kinds of beans, rocks, seeds – Helps to notice likenesses and differences, work with concepts, more and less;
- Water Activities: Pouring, sink and float, wet and dry, ...;
- Blocks Building: Learning to share with others while using imagination to create through building with blocks.

More Growing Exercises

These activities give the child an understanding of his personal care, as well as care of the environment around him. Children enjoy practical activities that make the environment beautiful. They build up self-esteem when they are involved in these activities. Self-help skills also develop the child's physical capabilities:

1. <u>Care of Person: Grooming</u>:

    ⇨ How to wash their face and hands;
    ⇨ How to brush their teeth;
    ⇨ How to blow their nose;
    ⇨ How to care for their hair.

    ☺ <u>Skills:</u> Taking Care of Self; Independence and Confidence.

    ✂ <u>Materials To Be Used:</u> Basin for water, soap; pictures of how to properly brush teeth; tissue to show child how to wipe nose properly and throw away dirty tissue; comb and brush to demonstrate proper hair care (do not let children share comb and brush). The skills mentioned above are important. Each Teacher will have to adapt the best way to present these skills.

    ✎ <u>Teacher's Notes:</u> Discussion on results of activity; open format; Teacher records own results.

More Growing Exercises

2. <u>Care of Person: Dressing:</u>

    ⇨ Teach child how to button, zip, snap, and tie;

    ☺ <u>Skills:</u> Personal Independence and Confidence.

    ✄ <u>Materials To Be Used:</u> A child's coat or sweater for buttoning, or snapping, or zipping; a child's shoe for tying.

    ✎ <u>Teacher's Notes:</u> Discussion on results of activity; open format; Teacher records own results.

More Growing Exercises

3. <u>Care of Environment: Sweeping:</u>

    ⇨ A small area is marked off. A child-sized broom and dustpan are placed in the area. The child is shown how to sweep and gather up the dirt.

☺ <u>Skills:</u> Taking care of the environment; Awareness of environment.

✂ <u>Materials To Be Used:</u> Child-size broom, made with a short piece of wood with stiff bristles tied on; a small dust pan, made with a stiff piece of cardboard (top of shoe box with one side cut out would work).

✎ <u>Teacher's Notes:</u> Discussion on results of activity; open format; Teacher records own results.

More Growing Exercises

4. <u>Care of Environment: Dusting:</u>

    ⇨ In a small box place 2 or 3 dust cloths. Show children how to dust shelves and equipment. When they are finished they should shake the cloth (out window or door), fold the cloth, and return it to the box. This dusting activity is opened for a child to do as the Teacher designates.

☺ <u>Skills:</u> Taking care of the environment; Awareness of environment.

✂ <u>Materials To Be Used:</u> Box; Small cloths.

✎ <u>Teacher's Notes:</u> Discussion on results of activity; open format; Teacher records own results.

More Growing Exercises

5. <u>Plant and Garden Care: Flower Arranging:</u>

   A variety of vases in different sizes and shapes should be kept in the classroom. One or two small, shallow containers will be needed as children sometimes snip the flower stalk until only the flower is left. When this happens the flowers can be turned into a floating arrangement.

   It is hoped that the school can grow flowers with the children. If there is no garden, a long planter box can be used. Children should be taught how to cut flowers for flower arrangements. They are shown how to cut a flower with a reasonable length of stem without including buds, as these need to be left on the plant to bloom later. For example, roses should be cut with a slanting cut about ½ inch above a bud that points out of the bush. In this way, the correct shape of the bush is maintained.

   The child covers the table with newspaper and fills the vase nearly full of water. The teacher shows the child how to strip the leaves off that part of the stem that will go into the water (If the leaves go into the water they will rot and the flowers will soon die.).

   The Teacher shows him how to snip one very small piece off each flower stalk and to place the flowers in the vase in a pleasing way. The Teacher leaves him to finish and to clear away any pieces. These will be put in the compost heap.

   <u>N.B.:</u> Very little children are inclined to snip pieces off the stalk until only a flower head is left. This can be floated in a shallow dish. Another lesson can be given another day stressing the fact that only one piece is snipped off the end of the stem.

   Children learn to care for the flowers, checking the water level in each vase daily and to give water to plants as necessary. They learn the right amount to give to each plant, as over-watering does harm. Potted plants are sold with instructions on their care included. The children can follow these. A small book on the care of indoor plants should be kept in the classroom and referred to by the Teacher and children.

More Growing Exercises

Plant and Garden Care: Flower Arranging (Continued):

When flowers are out of season, leaves, twigs, and berries (non-poisonous) can be arranged. Some plants can be grown in the garden for the beauty of their leaves. Dried grasses, dried flowers, and dried flower parts can be collected and used in winter decorations.

☺ Skills: Observation of nature; Taking care of a garden; Cutting and arranging skills.

✂ Materials To Be Used: Newspaper, scissors, suitable flower vase, seeds, flowers, leaves, berries, plants.

✎ Teacher's Notes: Discussion on results of activity; open format; Teacher records own results.

More Growing Exercises

6. <u>Plant and Garden Care: The Garden:</u>

   All tools must be functional, strong, and of the right size for the children.

   There should be a compost heap. The children learn to sweep and tidy the yard, putting dead leaves, earth, etc., on the compost heap. Children can water as necessary, giving the right amount to each plant. Children can learn to weed, cut off dead leaves and flowers, and care for plants generally.

   There should be a patch of ground where the children dig the soil, rake, and plant seeds. They will care for the plants and grow vegetables and fruit.

   It would be ideal to have a few fruit trees such as an apple, plum, peach, and walnut.

   Little children are given seeds that grow quickly to plant. They are shown how to crumble the soil finely, to rake it smooth, to place the line, and make a furrow of the right depth for the seeds being planted. They are shown how to plant the seeds thinly in the case of small seeds, and the right distance apart in the case of larger ones. They are shown how to cover the seeds with earth and pat the row firmly. Some soils may then need watering with a fine spray. In the case of very small seeds, it is wise to mix them with a little sand or fine earth before planting, as this makes it easier to sow them thinly. The directions on the seed packet should be read and followed.

   Radishes and a quick growing lettuce can soon be cropped. Children should be able to pick some of the vegetables used in the exercises of practical life and for snack. They can also cut flowers and leaves for flower arrangements from the garden.

   On different occasions lessons are given on the use of each garden tool. The children must have adequate opportunities to practice the use of each tool.

More Growing Exercises

Plant and Garden Care: The Garden (Continued):

☺ <u>Skills:</u> The children are taught to recognize each type of weed, one at a time, and how to dig them up by the roots without damaging surrounding plants. Some can be pulled up by hand. Some need a dibble for long rooted ones.

The children learn how to cut off dead flowers and leaves in the right way for the different plants.

They learn how to water and when to water. They learn how to prepare the ground and plant different kinds of seeds. They learn how to plant out seedlings. The children learn to cut flowers, leaves, etc., for indoor use.

✄ <u>Materials To Be Used:</u> Yard brooms, fork, rake, watering cans, garden twine and stakes, trowel, hand fork, dibble, line, garden scissors, container for weeds (small wheelbarrow), hoe, a book on gardening.

✎ <u>Teacher's Notes:</u> Discussion on results of activity; open format; Teacher records own results.

More Growing Exercises

7. <u>General Growing Exercises: Managing Plastic Food Containers:</u>

   ⇨ The child sits at a table and is given two or three plastic food containers. He is shown how to remove the lids and put them on again. This requires practice and judgement of size.

   On different days he is shown how to use the containers with different types of caps.

   ✂ <u>Materials To Be Used:</u> Plastic food containers of different shapes with lids and caps of different sizes and types.

   ☺ <u>Skills:</u> Understanding how to open and close containers; Independence; Preparation for the Growing Exercises; and, as listed at front of Growing Exercises Section.

   ✎ <u>Teacher's Notes:</u> Discussion on results of activity; open format; Teacher records own results.

More Growing Exercises

8. <u>General Growing Exercises: Managing Bottles with Screw Tops:</u>

    ⇨ The child is given a bottle with a screw top and shown how to unscrew the top and screw it on again. On different days, as he is ready, he is shown how to manage the different fastenings. These are kept on a shelf for him to take and use.

    ✂ <u>Materials To Be Used:</u> A collection of bottles and containers with screw tops or corks or other fastenings used on household containers. Empty household containers can be collected after the contents have been used.

    ☺ <u>Skills:</u> Understanding how to open and close containers; Independence.

    ✎ <u>Teacher's Notes:</u> Discussion on results of activity; open format; Teacher records own results.

More Growing Exercises

9. <u>General Growing Exercises: Managing Plastic Containers That "Squeeze"</u>:

    ⇨   The child is given a container full of water. He stands in front of the sink and squeezes a little liquid at a time out of the container into the sink.

    ✂ <u>Materials To Be Used:</u> Plastic containers that squeeze to eject a liquid.

    ☺ <u>Skills:</u> Independence; Hand co-ordination.

    ✎ <u>Teacher's Notes:</u> Discussion on results of activity; open format; Teacher records own results.

More Growing Exercises

10. <u>General Growing Exercises: Learning To Use a Spoon:</u>

    ⇨ The child has the tray with a dish of rice and an empty dish and a spoon in front of him. The child is shown how to hold the spoon and transfer the rice spoonful by spoonful into the empty dish without spilling any. If he spills he can be shown how to clear up afterwards. He spoons rice from one dish to the other until satisfied.

    Any one of these commodities (rice, lentils, small beans or dried peas) can be kept available for this exercise. The child can help himself to a tray, dishes and a spoon, and choose a commodity to work with.

    <u>Variation:</u> When the child can do this exercise without spilling, he can spoon water from one bowl to another without spilling.

☺ <u>Skills:</u> Hand and Eye co-ordination: Independence.

✂ <u>Materials To Be Used:</u> A tray; Two attractive dishes; A small spoon; Uncooked rice, lentils, small beans or dried peas.

✎ <u>Teacher's Notes:</u> Discussion on results of activity; open format; Teacher records own results.

More Growing Exercises

11. <u>General Growing Exercises: Pouring</u>:

    ⇨ The child is shown how to hold the pitcher of rice (lentils) with the lip just over the empty pitcher. He is told not to let the pitchers touch each other when he is pouring (the lips of the pitchers might get chipped). He is shown how to tilt the pitcher he is holding slowly until the rice (lentils) pour into the empty pitcher. He practices pouring from one pitcher to another.

    <u>Subsequent Exercises:</u>

    ⇨ When the child is able to pour solids without spilling, he can pour water from one pitcher to another;

    ⇨ A tray with a pitcher of liquid and a bottle or container with a small neck plus funnel. The child is shown how to pour liquid down the funnel until the bottle or container is full.

    ⇨ Pouring liquid into cups or glasses. The child has two or three cups or glasses on a tray and practices pouring liquid into each without spilling or over filling;

    ⇨ The child can practice pouring, using a large jug or bottle. The Teacher shows him how to hold the jug by the handle with his dominant hand and support the bottom of the jug with the other hand when pouring;

    ⇨ When he can pour successfully, he can serve water, milk or juice to the children at lunchtime.

In all these exercises, the lip of the pitcher must be just over and above the vessel into which the liquid is to be poured. The pitcher and the vessel must not touch.

☺ <u>Skills:</u> Pouring without spilling, and as listed at front of Growing Exercises Section.

✂ <u>Materials To Be Used:</u> Two small, attractive pitchers; A tray; Rice or lentils in one of the pitchers, three-quarters full.

✎ <u>Teacher's Notes:</u> Discussion on results of activity; open format; Teacher records own results.

More Growing Exercises

12. <u>General Growing Exercises: Dry Measure - Spoons:</u>

    ⇨ Collect a set of Measuring Spoons, a container with flour, a blunt knife, and an empty container on a tray;

    ⇨ The child is shown how to take one Measuring Spoon and fill it with flour. He is shown how to take the blunt knife with his dominant hand, and, holding the spoon of flour over the flour container, level it off with the knife and put the measured flour in the empty container;

    ⇨ This work needs to be done carefully and exactly. No flour should be spilled. Any Measuring Spoon can be used for practice.

    ⇨ <u>Additional Exercise:</u> Lessons can be given with Measuring Cups in the same manner.

☺ <u>Skills:</u> The child learns the appropriate words for different size measuring spoons. While using the measuring spoons his attention is drawn to the amounts and the way they are used.

✂ <u>Materials To Be Used:</u> Set of Measuring Spoons; A container with Flour; A blunt knife; An empty container.

✐ <u>Teacher's Notes:</u> Discussion on results of activity; open format; Teacher records own results.

More Growing Exercises

13. <u>General Growing Exercises: Liquid/Dry Measure Containers:</u>

    ⇨ <u>Exercise: 2 Cups = 1 Pint; 2 Pints = 1 Quart; 4 Quarts = 1 Gallon:</u>

    The child has the cup and pint containers at the sink. He is shown how to fill a measure exactly without spilling. He is asked to find the number of times a cup can be filled and emptied into the pint. He fills the cup and empties it into the pint container until the pint is full. He finds that 2 cups equal a pint. Most children repeat this a great many times.

    Another time the same can be done with the pint and quart, then with the quart and gallon. After that the child can take all the containers and practice. The measures are kept in the classroom for him to use in this way. He is encouraged to work carefully and not spill water or over-fill the containers.

    <u>Note:</u> If a sink and water are not available, fine rice or sand can be used for pouring. A large empty container to pour over can be placed on a table or on the floor next to the container of sand or rice. Then the empty measuring containers may also be available for filling.

    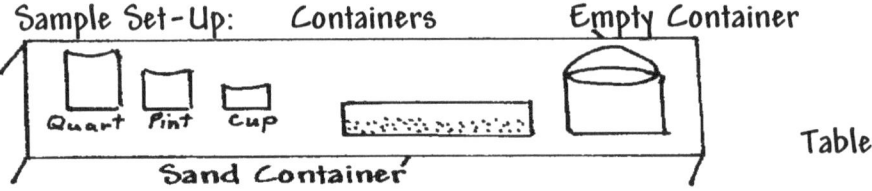

    ☺ <u>Skills:</u> The child learns the appropriate words for cup, pint, quart, and gallon. While doing the exercises with the containers his attention is drawn to the way these terms are used. For example, we buy a quart of milk. The measures can be shown in recipes.

    ✄ <u>Materials To Be Used:</u> Cup, pint, quart, and gallon measuring containers, preferably with a lip.

    ✎ <u>Teacher's Notes:</u> Discussion on results of activity; open format; Teacher records own results.

More Growing Exercises

Cooking Recipes

1. <u>Fried Bread</u>

1 cup flour	2 teaspoons baking powder
1 cup whole wheat flour	½ teaspoon salt

   Mix ingredients with enough warm water to form dough like pie crust. Knead until pliable. Pat and flatten pieces of dough into 8" circles. The thinner the dough is, the better the Fried Bread is. Heat 1" of oil in a hot skillet. Fry dough until lightly browned on one side. Turn and brown other side. Drain on paper towels. Eat with honey or maple syrup.

2. <u>Lemonade</u>

1 cup water	¾ tablespoon sugar
1 ½ tablespoons lemon juice	ice

   Cut and squeeze lemons to obtain lemon juice. Combine juice with water and sugar. Add ice and serve.

3. <u>Potato Salad</u>

4 cups diced cooked potatoes	1 cup mayonnaise
3 diced hard-cooked eggs	1 cup diced celery

   Mix mayonnaise or sour cream in a bowl with potatoes and eggs. Add salt to taste. Cool. Serve.

4. <u>Corn Chips</u>

1 cup boiling water	½ teaspoon salt
¼ cup margarine	1 cup cornmeal

   Combine first three ingredients. Add cornmeal. Make into 1" balls. Place on lightly greased cookie sheet. Spread with spoon or pat with fingers until very thin. Bake at 350° for 20 minutes, or until crisp and golden brown. Enjoy hot or cold.

More Growing Exercises (Cooking Recipes Continued)

5. <u>Banana Bread</u>

   ½ cup shortening
   1 cup sugar
   2 eggs
   1 cup mashed bananas
       (3 large bananas)

   1 teaspoon lemon juice
   2 cups flour
   1 ½ baking powder
   ¼ teaspoon salt
   ½ teaspoon baking soda

   Cream shortening and sugar. Blend in beaten eggs and mashed bananas. Add milk and lemon juice. Add flour sifted with salt, baking powder and baking soda. Bake in greased loaf pan at 350 - 375° for 50-60 minutes.

6. <u>Egg Nog Drink</u>

   2 cups milk
   2 eggs

   2 tablespoons sugar
   ½ teaspoon vanilla

   Beat eggs and other ingredients together. Serve cold.

7. <u>Fruit Salad</u>

   Choose local fruits in season. Show children how to clean and cut the fruit into bite-sized pieces. Mix together in a bowl.

   Fruit Salad is great with a slice of Banana Bread and a glass of Lemonade. Add Potato Salad for a full meal!

Extended Growing Exercises
(For Older Children)

1. <u>Dressing</u>

    ⇨ Use of Dressing Frames to practice Dressing Skills such as: Buttons, Snaps, Hooks, Buckles, Bows, Lacing, Zippers, Safety Pins, Fasteners on Overalls, etc.;

    ⇨ Use of apron;

    ⇨ Dressing for change of weather;

    ⇨ Putting on pullover sweatshirt;

    ⇨ Putting on boots.

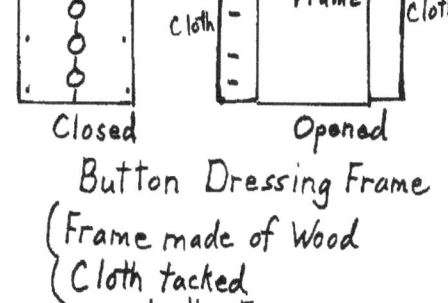

Button Dressing Frame
(Frame made of Wood
(Cloth tacked to the Frame

2. <u>Care of Clothing</u>

    ⇨ Polishing shoes;

    ⇨ Washing, drying, and folding of clothes;

    ⇨ Sewing on buttons;

    ⇨ Sewing ripped seam;

    ⇨ Use of coat rack;

    ⇨ How to hang clothes on a hanger;

    ⇨ Rolling socks;

    ⇨ Ironing clothes (older children).

3. <u>Grooming</u>

    ⇨ Washing hands;

    ⇨ Washing face;

    ⇨ Washing hair;

    ⇨ Brushing teeth/Flossing teeth;

    ⇨ Buffing fingernails;

    ⇨ Cleaning fingernails;

    ⇨ Cutting nails;

    ⇨ Blowing nose;

    ⇨ Combing hair;

    ⇨ Cleaning cuts and bandaging them.

Extended Growing Exercises (Continued)

4. <u>Care of Environment</u>

    ⇨ Sharpening pencils;
    ⇨ Cleaning paint brushes;
    ⇨ Mixing paint;
    ⇨ Cleaning erasers;
    ⇨ Cleaning spills;
    ⇨ Sweeping;
    ⇨ Returning things to where they belong;
    ⇨ Washing tables/chairs/door/sink;
    ⇨ Dusting with cloth;
    ⇨ Polishing silver, brass, wood, mirrors;
    ⇨ Sweeping carpets;
    ⇨ Sweeping floor;
    ⇨ Washing cleaning cloths;
    ⇨ Using sponges;
    ⇨ Use of dustpan and bush;
    ⇨ Moving furniture;
    ⇨ Floor scrubbing;
    ⇨ Cleaning shells or rocks;
    ⇨ Straightening shelves;
    ⇨ Taking care of pets.

Extended Growing Exercises (Continued)

5. <u>Plant and Garden Care</u>

    ⇨ Watering according to the needs of plants;
    ⇨ Washing leaves;
    ⇨ Repotting plants;
    ⇨ Planting seeds;
    ⇨ Fertilizing;
    ⇨ Cleaning drainage dishes;
    ⇨ Arranging flowers;
    ⇨ Changing water in vases;
    ⇨ Washing vases;
    ⇨ Using shovel to turn over the soil;
    ⇨ Pruning;
    ⇨ Raking leaves;
    ⇨ Staking plants and flowers;
    ⇨ Pulling weeds;
    ⇨ Cutting off dead material;
    ⇨ Watering.

6. <u>Food Preparation</u>

    ⇨ Washing vegetables;
    ⇨ Slicing, chopping, grating, spreading;
    ⇨ Stirring, shaking, sifting;
    ⇨ Use of rolling pin;
    ⇨ Kneading;
    ⇨ Beating with fork or eggbeater;
    ⇨ Use of can opener;
    ⇨ Shelling peas;
    ⇨ Packing school lunch;
    ⇨ How to reseal boxes and opened jars.

Extended Growing Exercises (Continued)

7. <u>Feeding Self</u>

    ⇨ Spooning;
    ⇨ Use of utensils:
        ⇨ Pouring milk from pitcher;
        ⇨ Serving self and others;
    ⇨ Setting table;
    ⇨ Cleaning table;
    ⇨ Table etiquette;
    ⇨ Cleaning spills;
    ⇨ Dish washing and drying;
    ⇨ Cutting and serving;
    ⇨ Coffee grinding;
    ⇨ Peeling vegetables;
    ⇨ Napkin folding;
    ⇨ Pouring rice;
    ⇨ Sifting cornmeal.

8. <u>Fine Hand Development</u>

    ⇨ Scissors;
    ⇨ Knitting;
    ⇨ Crochet;
    ⇨ Weaving;
    ⇨ Needlepoint;
    ⇨ Macrame;
    ⇨ Braiding;
    ⇨ Tying knots;
    ⇨ Arranging flowers;
    ⇨ Opening/closing lids
    ⇨ Locking/unlocking locks;

Extended Growing Exercises (Continued)

Fine Hand Development (Continued)

- ⇨ Handling tools: Hammers, screw drivers, nuts and bolts;
- ⇨ Mixing colors using eye droppers;
- ⇨ Tweezers to sort beads;
- ⇨ Clothespins;
- ⇨ Water pouring from pitcher to pitcher;
- ⇨ Using a funnel with small-necked bottle;
- ⇨ Stringing beads;
- ⇨ Stapling;
- ⇨ Using hole punch;
- ⇨ Measuring liquids and solids;
- ⇨ Making a bed or cot;
- ⇨ Purses with different opening systems;
- ⇨ Use of rubber bands;
- ⇨ Pasting;
- ⇨ Use of pegboards;
- ⇨ Puzzles;
- ⇨ Scoop to sift corn or rice;
- ⇨ Using paring knife;
- ⇨ Grating soap or vegetables;
- ⇨ Sorting.

✎ Teacher's Notes: Discussion on results of activity; open format; Teacher records own results.

www.fortheloveofchildrenbook.com   E-mail: info@.fortheloveofchildrenbook.com

Part 3
Science - Nature

Science

In Science we learn
    About birds in the sky,
        And trees in the forest,
            And water flowing by;

We listen,
    And look,
        At the wonders around us,
            And discover new things
                That will surely astound us!

Vanessa Conaway Pace

Introduction To Science

Children are natural scientists. They are on an eager and endless pursuit to find out how the world works. Science is an easy topic to cover in the preschool classroom, once the teacher develops an awareness of what science really is for children between one and six years of age. We are the blessed ones, those of us who work with young children, because everything is new and wonderful and worthy of exploration to the young child.

Noticing

The first major task of the teacher is to help children *"notice"*. Young children are often so thorough in their investigation of any environment they find themselves in; that often all a teacher has to do is *notice with* a child. "Oh, look at this!" "You found something interesting."

Providing children with interesting things to notice is part of the teacher's role. Often, it seems, displays of natural objects on the science table do nothing but gather dust. One way to create new interest in "science stuff" is to use science table materials as centerpieces for the lunch table. Try putting the fish bowl or a collection of rocks or some shells in the middle of the table as children eat. The conversation will soon focus on what they see in front of them. Then the "science stuff" can be returned to the science table, where further conversation can take place. Placing two little chairs at the science table will encourage a couple of children to spend time together discussing what is displayed.

On-Going Nature Collection

An excellent alternative to the "bring and brag" type of show-and-tell is a nature show-and-tell. Encourage children to bring anything they find, such as rocks, shells, starfish, nuts, feathers, etc. Label each item museum-style as it is added to the collection. Example: "This is a rock named Ralph, found by Jason. On the balance scale we discovered that Ralph is as heavy as Jason's shoe. Jason found Ralph in a creek when he and his Mom went for a walk. When it is wet, it turns pretty colors." Children will enjoy having these descriptions read to them often.

Introduction To Science (Continued)

Science Scrapbook

Review is important. Since many science projects are a one-time experience, a scrapbook of science experiences is ideal. Use photographs, illustrations, child-dictated descriptions, pressed flowers and leaves, brochures from science-related field trips, etc. This will keep fresh in the child's memory the day the rabbit visited, what their adopted tree looked like in October, what went into the cake batter, how big the baby guinea pig was when you first got her, etc. The children enjoy having this read to them again and again, and it is also one way to show parents the depth of your program.

Sensory Perception

Sensory perception is the basis of all scientific investigation. Children "notice" things by seeing, smelling, hearing, tasting, and touching. Therefore, any classroom activities that give children opportunities to use their senses in an organized way are legitimate science activities. As children investigate any new object or phenomena we can encourage them to use several of their senses. "It's getting windy .... Listen. Close your eyes - do you feel the warm wind on your cheeks and in your hair? Look what it is doing to my scarf. It smells like trees, doesn't it?"

Sorting

Sorting things is one of the most basic and varied science activities we can offer children. Children must be able to notice details before they can sort things. When they sort they are classifying things, forming categories according to characteristics they perceive. This is the beginning of logical thought - a prerequisite, really.

Testing

Learning to make "educated guesses" is part of scientific thinking. There are many opportunities for this type of experience. "Which of these things do you think is heaviest?" "How many nuts do you think will fit into this jar?" "Which jar do you think will hold all of the nuts?"

Introduction To Science (Continued)

Labeling

Scientists like to name things and identify things accurately. So do children. Starting with the toddler game of "Whassat?", children are learning to represent things and phenomena with words. A large part of any science curriculum is vocabulary development. It starts with being able to name attributes – adjectives, in other words; hard, soft, hot, cold, blue, wet, rough, big, heavy, etc., etc., etc.

Children start with very broad categories. As their experience and vocabularies grow, categories become narrower and more defined. For instance, a toddler may call any four-legged animal "doggie". When he is corrected, "No, that is a cow," he may then call all large four-legged animals "cow" and all small ones "doggie". This is further refined as he finds out about deer, horses, cats, sheep, etc. This is a lifelong process.

An important role of the teacher is to provide the "envelope of language" for all science experiences. This does not necessarily mean identifying everything they see scientifically. There will be some older preschoolers who will enjoy learning long names of dinosaurs, types of rocks, and scientific names of insects. The major focus, however, will be on getting children to accurately describe what they see.

Changes

Science becomes alive and interesting when things change. When children notice changes, or make changes happen, that is when wheels start turning in their heads. "What is making that ice cube turn to water?" "If I change the angle of the board, will the ball roll down faster and go further?" Cooking projects (chemistry) almost all involve materials changing. Keep samples of all individual ingredients aside to compare with the finished product. How did it get that way? Can children reproduce changes – can they make it happen again? This is one indication of comprehension.

Introduction To Science (Continued)

Spontaneous versus Planned Science

Some of the best science experiences come about as a result of spontaneous unplanned happenings in a classroom. Someone finds a caterpillar. A parent surprises you with a visit from a mother cat and a litter of kittens. You discover a bird nesting under the eaves. Sometimes such events will cause you to put aside other plans for the day. Other times they can be worked into your regular plans. The important thing is to keep your awareness up so you can take advantage of all the possible science learnings in your environment.

What to Present

Preschoolers relate best to what they can see and perceive with their senses. Therefore, talking about "chloroplasts" that make leaves green, or magnetism forces, would not be as appropriate as things children encounter in nature. Try to relate your science experiences to the real world of the children in your group. Plants, animals, nature, the change of seasons, weather, cooking, simple machines like slides, pulleys, seesaws and swings, and gravity, are all possibilities.

Teaching Strategies

The term "Discovery Approach" is part of our professional jargon. It means not supplying all the answers, but allowing children to discover answers for themselves as much as possible.

A good way to introduce a topic is to say to the children, "Tell me everything you know about <u>shells</u> (whatever)." Write down what the children say. You will then be aware of their level of understanding and where they may have some misconceptions, and then you can build from there.

Children learn when they can "touch" and "do", rather than "listen" and "watch".

Introduction To Science (Continued)

Teaching Strategies (Continued)

Don't ask questions when you really want to give information. It is silly for an adult to ask a 3-year-old what color an apple is. First the child needs to be given the information. But do ask questions when you want to start children thinking: "What do you think this might be used for?" Use "open-ended" questions, rather than questions that have only one correct answer.

When children ask you a question, rather than immediately supplying the answer, try, "What do you think?" "Let's find out." "Let's test it and see." Of course, there will be times when it is appropriate to supply information.

Don't shelter children from making mistakes. Instead of saying, "If you make it too tall it will fall over," let the child make it too tall, and figure out how to stabilize it, or how to build it better when it does fall over.

Ask children to hypothesize – to guess what they think the results will be. Cooking will give you many opportunities for this. "What do you think will happen when we put these together?" Can children recall what they did – the steps in the process. "How did you make that?" "What did you need?" "What did you do first?" "Then what?"

Role of the Teacher

Your responsibility is to make sure children have frequent opportunities to explore new materials using all their senses. Allow children to sort, arrange, and randomly play with a wide variety of things. Take advantage of spontaneous science happenings. Encourage children to guess and test their guesses. Provide the all-important "envelope of language" around their science experiences. Most of all, model the enthusiasm and eagerness that is so natural to children in order to maximize their interest.

Science

Awareness of Self and the World Around Us

<u>Skills To Develop</u>

- New Vocabulary
- Using hands-on activities
- Learning through observation
- Sharing ideas
- Group things in categories
- Units:
    The Five Senses
    Seeds, Plants, Leaves
    Insects
    Animals and Their Babies
    Weather

<u>Activities - Overview</u>

Through discussion

Projects involving nature;
Collecting rocks, leaves, ...

Taking walks; Quiet times

What we saw, or collected, or experienced

Size, Shapes, Textures, Color, Weight
Growing A Garden

Experiencing The Weather

<u>Equipment:</u>

Use things in nature and environment for collecting; discussions; experimenting;
Weather Chart for Gathering (Circle) Time;
Jars, Containers for collecting; Milk cartons; Balance Scale.

<u>Objectives:</u>

- Awareness of ourselves;
- Awareness of things around us;
- Sameness and Differences of people and things: Large-Small, Light-Heavy, Tall-Short, ...;
- To answer questions - How, Why, Where, When;
- To appreciate nature and develop a sense of wonder;
- To make a loving, working relationship with each other.

Ideas for Room Arrangement: Science

Science Table

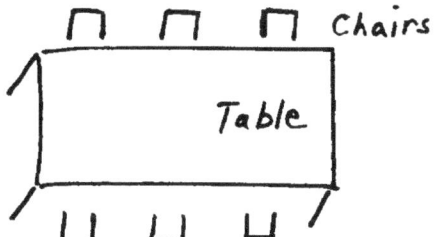

Display Nature Collections;
i.e., Rocks, Leaves, ...;
Children's Science Art Work:
Collages; Seeds; Leaves; ...

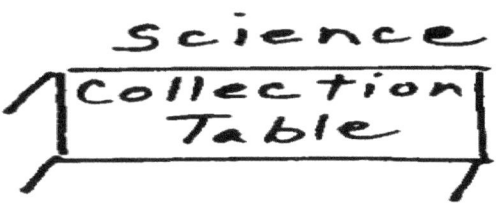

Science Shelf –
Look at Magazines -- Books

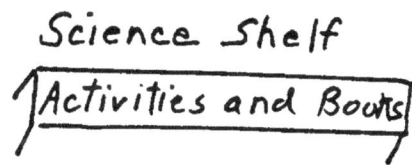

Science Areas
May be set up
Anyplace in the room.

More Activities:

- Art Nature Collages;
- Nature Walks to collect and talk about flowers, leaves, ...;
- Weather pictures – Discussions;
- Water Play – Hot/Cold; Wet/Dry; Sink/Float; Pouring; Empty/Full.

Science Projects

1. <u>Animal, Bird, or Fish:</u>

    ⇨ Mount three envelopes on large piece of cardboard.
    ⇨ Glue picture on each envelope to designate category.
    ⇨ Provide pictures of animals, birds, or fish.
    ⇨ Sort into proper categories.

☺ <u>Skills:</u> Listed at front of Science Section.

✂ <u>Materials To Be Used:</u> Cardboard backing, envelopes, paste, magazines with Animal, Bird, or Fish pictures, scissors.

✐ <u>Teacher's Notes:</u> Discussion on results of activity; open format; Teacher records own results.

Science Projects

2. <u>Nature Hunt:</u>

    ⇨ Go outside and collect leaves, rocks, grasses, flowers.
    ⇨ Let each child collect several items during Nature Walk.
    ⇨ In classroom, or outside, have a "gathering time".
    ⇨ Let children share with others what they have collected.
    ⇨ Let each child put an item on the classroom Science Table.

☺ <u>Skills:</u> Listed at front of Science Section.

✄ <u>Materials To Be Used:</u> Bags for collecting;

✐ <u>Teacher's Notes:</u> Discussion on results of activity; open format; Teacher records own results.

Science Projects

3. <u>How Big Is a STICK?</u>:

   ⇨ Is it longer than your arm?
   ⇨ Is it longer than your body?
   ⇨ Can you put the sticks together from largest to smallest?
   ⇨ Can you put the sticks together from smallest to largest?
   ⇨ Can you find a stick as long as your arm? Leg? Hand?
   ⇨ How many "hand" sticks does it take to make a "leg" stick?
   ⇨ How many "arm" sticks does it take to make a "leg" stick?
   ⇨ How big around are sticks?
   ⇨ Is it as big around as your arm?
   ⇨ Is it as big around as your fist?
   ⇨ Put the sticks in order by how round they are from fattest to thinnest;
   ⇨ How big a piece of string does it take to go around a stick?
   ⇨ If rulers are available, how thick is a stick?
   ⇨ How long is a crooked stick? (Use string to find out.)
   ⇨ What can you measure with a stick?
   ⇨ Can you measure a shadow?
   ⇨ Can you measure a tree?
   ⇨ Can you measure other sticks?
   ⇨ How are sticks the same?
   ⇨ How are sticks different?
   ⇨ Can you build with sticks?
   ⇨ Things to do:
      ⇨ Go on a stick hunt and find as many as you can;
      ⇨ How many of them were the same length?
      ⇨ Did you have one as long as you are tall?
      ⇨ Use a ruler to find how long each of the sticks really is;
      ⇨ Did you find a crooked stick that was about as long as a straight stick?

Science Projects

How Big Is a STICK? (Continued):

- ⇨ Try to find a stick that is as long as your leg;
- ⇨ Are any of the sticks as big around as your wrist?
- ⇨ Did you find a stick that was so long and big around that you could not lift it?
- ⇨ See what you can build with your sticks.

☺ <u>Skills:</u> Listed at front of Science Section.

✂ <u>Materials To Be Used:</u> Sticks.

✐ <u>Teacher's Notes:</u> Discussion on results of activity; open format; Teacher records own results.

Science Projects

4. <u>Flower Arranging:</u>

    ⇨ Children should be encouraged to bring cut flowers into classroom and arrange them in a jar – watering them daily – caring for them.

☺ <u>Skills:</u> Listed at front of Science Section.

✂ <u>Materials To Be Used:</u> A variety of jars – vases in different sizes and shapes to be kept in classroom; Shallow containers for "snipped" flower stalk where only flower is left; Scissors.

✎ <u>Teacher's Notes:</u> Discussion on results of activity; open format; Teacher records own results.

Science Projects

5. <u>Long Planter Box or Small Garden Spot:</u>

   ⇨ Children prepare soil – digging, cleaning out weeds;
   ⇨ After preparing the soil each child should help in planting seeds;
   ⇨ Children see to the daily care of the seeds, watering, etc.

☺ <u>Skills:</u> Listed at front of Science Section.

✂ <u>Materials To Be Used:</u> Digging materials (spoons, forks, small shovels, rakes); Watering cans; Seeds.

✎ <u>Teacher's Notes:</u> Discussion on results of activity; open format; Teacher records own results.

Science Projects

6. <u>Is It Full?</u>:

    ⇨   Start with a see-through container;

    ⇨   Fill container with large stones, and ask the children, "Is it full?" They will naturally respond, "It is full."

    ⇨   Then add small pebbles to the container with the large stones. They will filter down into the spaces between the rocks. Ask again, "Is it full?" They will naturally respond, "It is full."

    ⇨   Next, add sand or fine dirt to the container with the large stones and pebbles, all the way to the top, and once again ask, "Is it full?" The children will be *sure* that it is full this time.

    ⇨   Next, get a pitcher of water and *slowly* start to pour water in;

    ⇨   When the water reaches the top, once again ask, "Is it full?"

    ⇨   The container is now completely full!

☺ <u>Skills:</u> Listed at front of Science Section.

✂ <u>Materials To Be Used:</u> See-through Container; Rocks; Pebbles; Sand or Fine Dirt; Water.

✎ <u>Teacher's Notes:</u> Discussion on results of activity; open format; Teacher records own results.

Science Projects

7. <u>Sink and Float:</u> Provide a variety of objects that sink or float, and a container of water. Experiment with the following:

   ⇨ Which objects sink?
   ⇨ Which objects float?
   ⇨ Can you make something that sinks, float? (This can be accomplished by placing a small rock on a sponge.)

☺ <u>Skills:</u> Listed at front of Science Section.

✂ <u>Materials To Be Used:</u> A container with water in it. Sink objects - rocks, nails; Float objects - sponge, leaves, grasses, plastic lids.

✏ <u>Teacher's Notes:</u> Discussion on results of activity; open format; Teacher records own results.

Science Projects

8. <u>Rope Knowledge:</u> Have a rope about six feet long.

   Discuss the rope:

   ⇨ What words can be used to describe the rope?
   ⇨ What color is it?
   ⇨ Is it little or big?
   ⇨ Is it rough or smooth?
   ⇨ Is it round or square?
   ⇨ Is it long or short?
   ⇨ Can it make a noise?
   ⇨ What can you do with it?

   Ask a child to do any of the following:

   ⇨ Make a long or short line. Walk on the line, or jump on the line.
   ⇨ Make a circle or square with the rope.
   ⇨ Make a circle with the rope. Stand inside, stand outside, walk around the circle. Touch the circle with fingers, or toes, or elbows.

This is a fun game to play with children during Gathering (Circle) Time, letting each child have a turn.

☺ <u>Skills:</u> Listed at front of Science Section.

✂ <u>Materials To Be Used:</u> One Rope, at least 5 or 6 feet long.

✎ <u>Teacher's Notes:</u> Discussion on results of activity; open format; Teacher records own results.

Science Projects

9. <u>Balance Board:</u> Make balance board similar to a teeter-totter by using small board and a brick to balance the board in the center. Experiment with the following:

    ⇨ Place 2 objects on the Balance Board and maintain a balance;

    ⇨ Place many objects (rocks, wood, ---) on the board and maintain a balance.

☺ <u>Skills:</u> Listed at front of Science Section.

✂ <u>Materials To Be Used:</u> 1 Brick; 1 Board plank about 3 feet long, and wide enough to hold objects; 2 small cans (to place weight objects like rocks in). Cans will be placed on Balance Board with collected objects in them.

✎ <u>Teacher's Notes:</u> Discussion on results of activity; open format; Teacher records own results.

Science Projects

10. <u>Weighing Game:</u>

    ⇨ Make scales;
    - ⇨ Place 2 thick sticks on a table, with half of the stick extended off the edge of the table, and a brick holding the other end of each stick down on the table;
    - ⇨ Hang the Milk Cartons from the ends of the Sticks, close to the end (see drawing). At this point both "scales" should be hanging at exactly the same level;

    ⇨ Collect small items to be weighed;

    ⇨ Show child how to gently place items in the baskets;

    ⇨ Observe what is heavy and what is light;

    ⇨ Have the child try to even out the hanging baskets by adding and subtracting items.

☺ <u>Skills:</u> Listed at front of Science Section.

✂ <u>Materials To Be Used:</u> 2 Thick Sticks (1/2 inch wide and 1 foot long); 2 Bricks; 4 Rubber bands; String; Milk Cartons with the tops cut off; Items for weighing (rice, rocks, beans).

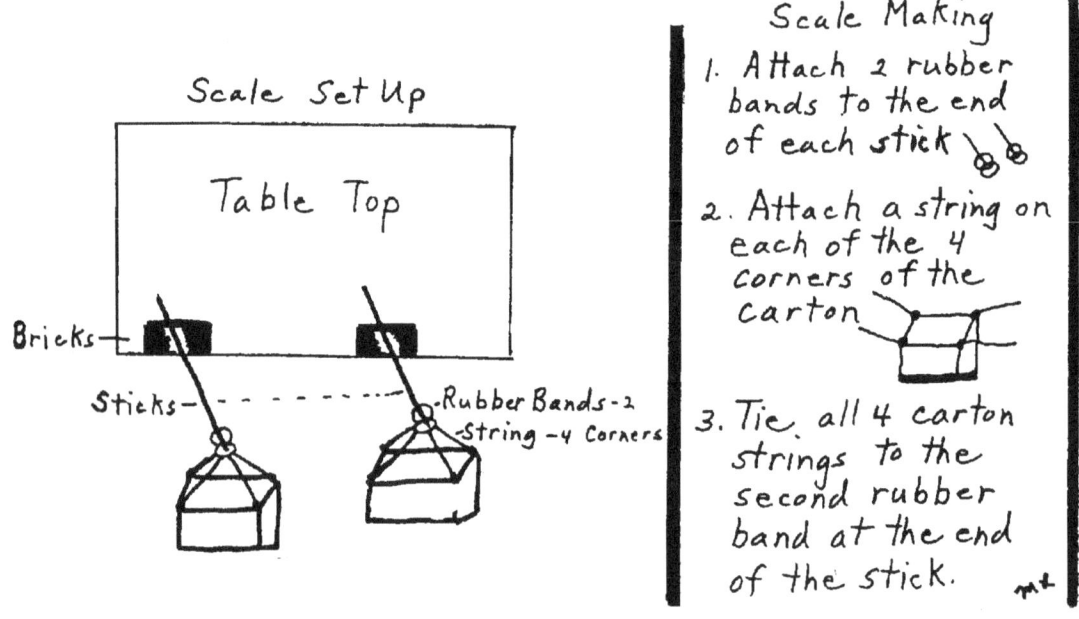

✐ <u>Teacher's Notes:</u> Discussion on results of activity; open format; Teacher records own results.

Science Projects

11. <u>Weather: What Makes the Rain?</u>: The biggest source for rain is the ocean. Lakes and other water bodies also contribute to the formation of rain. The heat from the sun causes water to evaporate from these water bodies and rise into the atmosphere, where it is condensed into clouds. Precipitation is produced when the tiny water droplets become too heavy to float, so they fall to earth in the form of rain, snow, sleet, or hail.

    ⇨ Place a tea kettle on a hot plate or stove, or over a fire;
    ⇨ When the water boils show the children the cloud that forms just beyond the spout;
    ⇨ Point out that the clear area near the spout is steam;
    ⇨ Hold a pie pan filled with ice cubes in the cloud;
    ⇨ What happens when the water vapor comes in contact with the pan?
    ⇨ Why?
    ⇨ Song: "Rain, Rain, Go Away"

    Rain, rain go away.
    Come again some other day.
    All the children want to play.
    Rain, rain go away.

☺ <u>Skills:</u> Listed at front of Science Section.

✄ <u>Materials To Be Used:</u> A jar; Ice.

✎ <u>Teacher's Notes:</u> Discussion on results of activity; open format; Teacher records own results.

Science Projects

12. <u>Weather: Air Contains Water</u>:

    ⇨ Discuss that air contains water;
    ⇨ Make certain the outside of a jar is dry;
    ⇨ Fill jar with ice cubes;
    ⇨ What happens?
    ⇨ How did water get on the outside of the jar?
    ⇨ Why? The air around the jar was cooled, forming water vapor.

☺ <u>Skills:</u> Listed at front of Science Section.

✂ <u>Materials To Be Used:</u> A jar; Ice.

✎ <u>Teacher's Notes:</u> Discussion on results of activity; open format; Teacher records own results.

Science Projects

13. <u>Weather: Evaporation:</u> When water is heated it evaporates (changes from liquid to gas) and becomes water vapor, or steam. Experiment with the following:

   ⇨ Sometimes the water vapor from evaporation can be seen.
   - ⇨ Observe steam from boiling water.
   - ⇨ Observe the water vapor from a cool mist vaporizer;

   ⇨ Sometimes the evaporation cannot be seen. For example, water evaporating from a lake cannot be seen. This water rises and forms clouds.
   - ⇨ Fill a pan to the top with water.
   - ⇨ Set the pan in a place where it will not be bumped;
   - ⇨ Mark the water level every morning;
   - ⇨ After a few days discuss what has happened to the water level, and why the water has evaporated.

   ⇨ Sometimes we can see the *results* of evaporation:

   <u>Drying fabrics in the sun:</u>
   - ⇨ Wash some doll clothes or handkerchiefs;
   - ⇨ Place them in the sun;
   - ⇨ What happens to the water?
   - ⇨ Do things dry quicker if spread out separately, or packed together?
   - ⇨ Wet six handkerchiefs. Roll three into a ball and place in sun. Lay remaining handkerchiefs separately and flat in the sun;
   - ⇨ Which dried quicker?
   - ⇨ Why? The warm air reaches all parts of the flat handkerchiefs, and the air surrounding them enhances the drying time.

Science Projects

Weather: Evaporation (Continued):

Chalkboard Experiment:
- ⇨ Wipe a chalkboard with a wet sponge;
- ⇨ Watch the water on the board disappear;
- ⇨ Where did it go?

Wet Hands Experiment:
- ⇨ Dip both hands in water;
- ⇨ Place one hand in front of a fan, or have another child fan it;
- ⇨ Which hand is cooler?
- ⇨ Why? The moving air causes evaporation. As the water evaporates it requires heat energy. This energy is drawn from the hand.

☺ Skills: Listed at front of Science Section.

✂ Materials To Be Used: A Pan for boiling water; Heat Source; Pie Pan; Handkerchiefs or lightweight Fabrics; Chalkboard; Sponge; Fan.

✐ Teacher's Notes: Discussion on results of activity; open format; Teacher records own results.

Science Projects

14. <u>Weather: What Makes Lightning?</u>: Lightning is a flash of light in the sky caused by energy (electricity) being released within a cloud, between a cloud and the ground, or between two clouds.

    ⇨ Go into a darkened room;
    ⇨ Rub two long, inflated balloons on clothing or fur;
    ⇨ Hold the balloons so they almost touch. A spark will jump between the two balloons. That spark is electricity. If the balloons had been clouds the sparks would have been lightning. Lightning is the electricity we see in the sky.
    ⇨ Or, run a comb through someone's fairly long hair. The sparks that you see are also electricity.

☺ <u>Skills:</u> Listed at front of Science Section.

✂ <u>Materials To Be Used:</u> Two long, inflated Balloons; Comb.

✎ <u>Teacher's Notes:</u> Discussion on results of activity; open format; Teacher records own results.

Science Projects

15. <u>Weather: What Makes Thunder?:</u> Thunder is a loud noise caused by lightning rapidly heating the air, which suddenly expands and contracts.

    ⇨ Inflate a paper bag and hold the neck tightly so air cannot escape;

    ⇨ Hit the bag with the other hand;

    ⇨ The bag will break with a loud bang. This causes the air in the bag to suddenly contract and expand, which makes the noise. This is how thunder occurs. It takes one second for thunder to go one mile. If the time between seeing the lightning and hearing the thunder is five seconds, the thunder is five miles away. When you see lightning and hear thunder at almost the same time, the storm is directly overhead.

    ⇨ Song: "I Hear Thunder" (Tune: "Frère Jacques"):

I hear thunder. I hear thunder. (Stamp feet on floor.)
Hark, don't you? Hark, don't you? (Place hand behind ear.)
Pitter patter raindrops. Pitter patter raindrops. (Wiggle fingers downward.)
I'm wet through. (Shake body.) So are you! (Point to friend.)

☺ <u>Skills:</u> Listed at front of Science Section.

✂ <u>Materials To Be Used:</u> A Paper Bag.

✎ <u>Teacher's Notes:</u> Discussion on results of activity; open format; Teacher records own results.

Science Projects

16. <u>Weather: What Makes a Rainbow?</u>: A rainbow is colored light seen in the sky when rays of the sun strike falling raindrops. Rainbows are curved because raindrops that reflect the sunlight are curved. Rainbows occur after a storm when the sun begins to shine while the air is still filled with raindrops. They occur most often in the morning or evening.

    Stripes of the rainbow are always red, orange, yellow, green, blue, and violet. (The order is easily remembered by the name "ROY G. BIV".) Sometimes one color may fade out (most often blue). The red is almost always seen. Sometimes two rainbows can be observed.

    A rainbow is really a circle that has no end. Occasionally passengers in low-flying aircraft see rainbows that form complete circles. The bottom half of the rainbow is hidden from most observers because it is below the horizon.

    Experiment with the following:

    <u>Mirror Rainbows</u>
    ⇨ Place a small mirror in a glass of water.
    ⇨ Place the glass of water so the sun will shine on the mirror;
    ⇨ Turn the glass until the rainbow is reflected against the wall;
    ⇨ Find the colors of the rainbow. The sun is made up of these colors. When sunlight hits raindrops or water the colors are separated.

    <u>Spray Rainbows</u>:
    ⇨ Spray a fine mist of water from a hose;
    ⇨ Stand with your back to the sun. A rainbow will appear in the fine spray of the water;
    ⇨ Stand with the spray between you and the sun;
    ⇨ Can you see the rainbow?
    ⇨ Why?

Science Projects

Weather: What Makes a Rainbow? (Continued):

Prism Rainbows:
- ⇨ A prism will separate colors just as the raindrops do.
- ⇨ Hold a prism to light and observe the colors;
- ⇨ Color a cardboard disk with the three primary colors on it in equal proportions;
- ⇨ Thread a string through the center of the disk;
- ⇨ Pull the ends of the string and spin the disk rapidly. The colors will combine, and the disk will appear to be white.

☺ Skills: Listed at front of Science Section.

✘ Materials To Be Used: A Mirror; A Glass of Water; A Hose; A Prism; Cardboard Disk; String; Sunlight.

✎ Teacher's Notes: Discussion on results of activity; open format; Teacher records own results.

Science Projects

17. <u>Weather: Wind:</u> Wind is moving air. Experiment with any of the following to create wind:

    ⇨ Blow with the mouth;
    ⇨ Fan with a large leaf or a piece of folded paper or cardboard;
    ⇨ Inflate a balloon and allow the air to escape through the opening;
    ⇨ Use an air pump;
    ⇨ Use a fan with several speeds;
    ⇨ Make a gentle breeze, and then a strong wind;
    ⇨ Discover what objects can be moved by the wind you create;
    ⇨ Make a chart of things the wind can do.

☺ <u>Skills:</u> Listed at front of Science Section.

✂ <u>Materials To Be Used:</u> A Fan, Air Pump, Large Leaf, or Piece of Folded Paper or Cardboard; Balloon.

✎ <u>Teacher's Notes:</u> Discussion on results of activity; open format; Teacher records own results.

Science Projects

18. <u>Seeds:</u>

   ⇨ Prepare a poster board display using pictures of fruits and vegetables cut from seed packages or seed catalogs;

   ⇨ Glue seed of each plant next to appropriate picture. For example: Glue peach seed beside picture of peach;

   ⇨ Provide a box of seeds that can be matched to seeds in the display;

   ⇨ Discuss how spring is the time that people plant seeds, from which most fruits and vegetables grow;

   ⇨ Discuss how seeds are different colors, sizes, and shapes. The size of the seed has nothing to do with the size of the plant that grows from it;

   ⇨ Discuss how each seed contains a tiny plant, food for the plant when it begins to grow, and a seed coat to help protect the plant. Take a seed apart and discover the different parts;

   ⇨ Discuss the fact that seeds are found in different "containers". Examples are pods, hard shells, and fruits.

☺ <u>Skills:</u> Listed at front of Science Section.

✂ <u>Materials To Be Used:</u> Various Seeds; Box; Poster Board; Pictures of Fruits and Vegetables.

✎ <u>Teacher's Notes:</u> Discussion on results of activity; open format; Teacher records own results.

Science Projects

19. <u>Plants: From Seed To Flower</u>:
    ⇨ Fold a large piece of paper in half. Fold in half again. Open paper.
    ⇨ In first section glue a seed
    ⇨ Rain is needed to make the seed grow. Draw rain in the second section;
    ⇨ The sun shines on the sprouted seed to help it grow. Draw a sun in the third section.
    ⇨ Soon the plant begins to flower. Draw a flower in the last section.

<u>Life Cycle of a Plant</u>:
    ⇨ Draw a large chart that displays the life cycle of a plant;
    ⇨ Discuss the plant's growth cycle:
        ⇨ First a seed is planted, which needs air, water, food, and sun to grow;
        ⇨ Next a small root grows from the seed;
        ⇨ Then a small shoot appears above the ground;
        ⇨ Drawing nourishment from the air, water, food, and sun, the young plant matures, developing leaves and flowers;
        ⇨ The flowers produce seeds, seed pods, or fruit. These seeds can be replanted, and the cycle is repeated.

☺ <u>Skills</u>: Listed at front of Science Section.

✄<u>Materials To Be Used</u>: Paper; Crayons or Colored Pencils; Seeds.

✎ <u>Teacher's Notes</u>: Discussion on results of activity; open format; Teacher records own results.

Science Projects

20. <u>Plant Parts: Flowers:</u>

    ⇨ Display a flower or plant, and discuss the different parts: The STEM supports the flower and leaves. It carries food from the roots to all parts of the plant;

    ⇨ The LEAVES are flat, thin, usually green blades growing out from the stem. LEAVES manufacture food for the plant with the help of sunlight;

    ⇨ The ROOTS are usually located beneath the ground. ROOTS anchor the plant. They also collect water and minerals from the soil for the plant;

    ⇨ The FLOWER is the seed-producing part of a flowering plant. A FLOWER contains petals, sepals, pistil, and stamens. The stamens hold pollen, which is a powder-like substance that is usually yellow.

<u>Plant Parts: Vegetables:</u>

   ⇨ Display vegetables, using pictures or real produce;
   ⇨ Discuss which part of each plant can be eaten:
       ⇨ STEM: Celery, rhubarb, asparagus;
       ⇨ LEAF: Cabbage, spinach, parsley, lettuce, kale, collard;
       ⇨ ROOT: Beets, carrots, radishes, turnips;
       ⇨ FLOWER: Broccoli, cauliflower;
       ⇨ SEED: Peas, beans, sunflower, pumpkin, peanut;
       ⇨ FRUIT: Eggplant, peppers, tomatoes, squash, okra, cucumbers, bananas;
       ⇨ BULB: Onion, garlic;
       ⇨ TUBER: Potato, sweet potato; yams.

☺ <u>Skills:</u> Listed at front of Science Section.

✂ <u>Materials To Be Used:</u> Samples or pictures of plants and flowers.

✎ <u>Teacher's Notes:</u> Discussion on results of activity; open format; Teacher records own results.

Science Projects

21. <u>Flower Identification:</u>

    ⇨ Display and pass around a variety of spring flowers. Flowers can be real or pictures;

    ⇨ Discuss name, color, shape, size, and smell of each flower;

    ⇨ Record descriptions on a piece of paper. For example: Let the children see, feel, and smell a flower, and then describe its blossoms. Record their descriptions.

☺ <u>Skills:</u> Listed at front of Science Section.

✂ <u>Materials To Be Used:</u> Samples and/or pictures of flowers; Paper; Pencil.

✎ <u>Teacher's Notes:</u> Discussion on results of activity; open format; Teacher records own results.

Science Projects

22. <u>Insect Information:</u>
    - Discuss and show pictures of insects:
        - Insects are the most numerous kind of animal in the world. They live everywhere on land, but only a few insects live in the ocean;
        - Insects are many different sizes, shapes, and colors. Fairy flies and some beetles are so small they can go through the eye of a needle. The largest insects are the Goliath beetle, which is four inches in length, and the Atlas moth, which has a wing spread of ten inches;
        - Beetles, grasshoppers, bees, wasps, butterflies, moths, ants, mosquitoes, flies, and ladybugs are some common insects;
        - Insects come from eggs. Baby insects are usually called larvae;
        - An insect has six legs and a jointed body which consists of three distinct parts: The head, thorax (or middle body), and abdomen. A good example of this is an ant;
        - Some insects have hooks and sticky pads on their feet which aid them in walking upside down or on smooth surfaces;
        - Most winged insects have four wings (two pairs).
        - Their antennae detect odors, sound waves, respond to air currents, and are used for touch;
        - Some insects are helpful. They produce foods we eat, pollinate plants, eat other insects which are harmful, and are a source of food for many animals;
        - Some insects are harmful. Mosquitoes, flies, and fleas spread disease. Other insects eat crops and destroy trees.

Science Projects

Insect Information (Continued):

⇨ Activities:
- ⇨ Go for a nature walk looking for insects;
- ⇨ Talk about where the insects live;
- ⇨ Collect insects for observation; (Be sure to release them at the end of the day!)

☺ Skills: Listed at front of Science Section.

✂ Materials To Be Used: Examples and/or Pictures of Insects; Containers for Collections.

✎ Teacher's Notes: Discussion on results of activity; open format; Teacher records own results.

www.fortheloveofchildrenbook.com   E-mail: info@.fortheloveofchildrenbook.com

Part 4
Mathematics

Mathematics

In Mathematics we Count,
    And we Touch,
        And we Feel,
            And we learn
                To match patterns
                    With things
                        That are real.

And we see
    There's a rhythm
        To patterns
            And sound,
                So we learn
                    To write numbers
                      For the things
                          That we've found!

Vanessa Conaway Pace

Introduction To Mathematics

We do our children a disservice when we make ourselves the major source of their knowledge. As important as we are in a child's life, we must realize that they acquire much of their knowledge on their own. Encouraging preschool children to Explore, Count, Pattern, Sort and Classify with real, familiar materials (rocks, buttons, shells, seeds, ...,) makes their learning fun, and increases their ability to learn.

Here are a few important points:

1. Children should be able to learn Mathematics from materials they are familiar with in real life;
2. Children should be able to share their Mathematics discoveries with their classmates;
3. Children should be allowed to use the Mathematics materials outside of the presentation time. Repeating the learned activities re-enforces the children's skills and interests.

Once Mathematics involves the child's "real world" it also becomes a part of his or her language and art development. The child who is encouraged to "Freely Explore," "Pattern," "Sort," and "Classify" materials becomes more observant of his environment. The child who can share discoveries while working with the simple math materials, develops language and art skills. Thoughts and ideas are also increased. What better way to help a child grow in the awareness and knowledge of the world around him?

Mathematics

Hands On Experience in Pre-Math Skills

Skills To Develop	Activities – Overview
• Sensorial Knowledge (Touch and Feel) is very important for Math.	"Hands-on" touch games
• Free Exploration	Treasure Boxes
• Patterning	Pattern Builder Cards
• Sorting and Classifying	Treasure Boxes
• Counting	Counting Forward, Counting Backward
• Sequence of Numbers	Flash Card with symbols
• Writing Numbers	Dotted trace-over number sheets; Crayons or Pencil

Equipment:

Treasure Boxes; Individual small table mat (paper or material)
Number Flash Cards with symbol on them

Objectives:

- Teaching children through concrete experience with "hands-on" materials
- Gradual introduction to materials;
- Joining concrete objects to symbols (1, 2, 3, ...);
- Learning counting from number chart or flash cards;
- Learning to share and enjoy math materials with those around you.

Ideas for Room Arrangement: Mathematics

Instruction should be given at the Tables.
(Each child receives one box and mat)

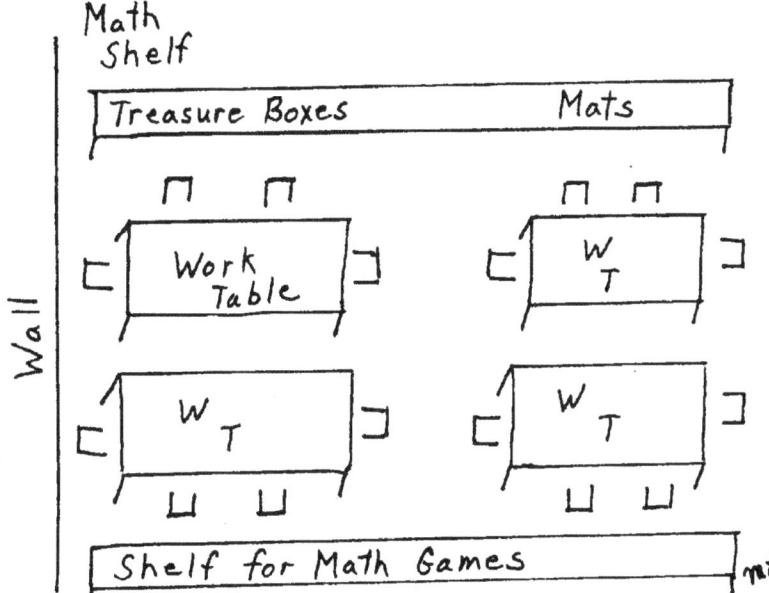

Math Area may be
Set up anyplace in
The room.

More Activities:

- Matching 2 sets of Number Cards - 1 to 5, then 1 to 10;
- Use your imagination to expand on ideas for - Exploration, Patterning, Sorting, Classifying, and Counting.

Mathematics

1. <u>Free Exploration: Treasure Boxes:</u> Children explore new materials in their own way.

    ⇨ Small boxes, each filled with materials a child can explore. This activity can be done by one child, or by a group of children with Teacher guiding them.

    ☺ <u>Skills:</u> Teaching children through concrete experience with hands on materials.

    ✂ <u>Materials To Be Used:</u> Rocks, seeds, buttons, for boxes; Small mat for each child to sort on.

    ✎ <u>Teacher's Notes:</u> Discussion on results of activity; open format; Teacher records own results.

Mathematics (Free Exploration Continued)

2. <u>Free Exploration: Treasure Pattern Cards:</u>

    ⇨ Child makes a pattern with material in Treasure Box on table. Then child draws on a card the pattern on the table. This activity can be done by one child, or by a group of children.

    ☺ <u>Skills:</u> Creating original patterns; Reproducing and extending patterns; Observing similarities and differences; Comparing and relating; Analyzing patterns.

    ✂ <u>Materials To Be Used:</u> Treasure boxes and pieces of tagboard or cardboard.

    ✎ <u>Teacher's Notes:</u> Discussion on results of activity; open format; Teacher records own results.

Mathematics

3. <u>Patterns: Rhythmic Clapping:</u> Patterning through simple hands-on activities prepares a child for abstract mathematical patterns later.

   ⇨ This is a group activity. The Teacher claps a pattern, and the child joins in. Children can suggest movements to do with clapping.

   Examples of Pattern: Clap, Clap (stop):   Clap, Clap (stop)
                                                 Clap, Clap, Snap: Clap, Clap, Snap

   ☺ <u>Skills:</u> Co-ordination; Rhythm; Remote preparation for reading the Pattern Cards.

   ✂ <u>Materials To Be Used:</u> None

   ✎ <u>Teacher's Notes:</u> Discussion on results of activity; open format; Teacher records own results.

Mathematics

4. <u>Patterns: The Dot Chart:</u>

   ➡ This is a group activity. During Gathering Time the Teacher holds a large dot chart on her lap and allows individual child to come up and continue to draw a pattern the Teacher has started.

   ☺ <u>Skills:</u> Children learn to reproduce and extend patterns. Left to right progression is strengthened also.

   ✂ <u>Materials To Be Used:</u>   Large "dot-to-dot" chart and a marking pen.

   Sample:

   ✎ <u>Teacher's Notes:</u> Discussion on results of activity; open format; Teacher records own results.

Mathematics

5. <u>Patterns: Dot Chart Patterns:</u>

   ⇨ This is an individual activity. Child may make own pattern cards by copying pattern from a dot-to-dot card.

   ☺ <u>Skills:</u> Children learn to reproduce and extend patterns. Left to right progression is strengthened also.

   ✂ <u>Materials To Be Used:</u> Dot pattern cards with patterns on them; Blank pattern cards for children to copy pattern on; Pens to make patterns.

   Sample: Sample Card   Blank Card

   ✐ <u>Teacher's Notes:</u> Discussion on results of activity; open format; Teacher records own results.

Mathematics

6. <u>Patterns: People Row Patterns:</u>

    ⇨   Rows of children make own patterns by standing - sitting:

    1 person stands, second one sits, etc.;
    2 people stand, second two sit, etc.;
    1 person stands, second two sit, etc.

    Children act out pattern and verbalize or draw results.

    ☺ <u>Skills:</u> Following Directions; Left-to-right Discrimination; Pattern Extension; Observing Similarities and Differences.

    ✂ <u>Materials To Be Used:</u> Paper, pencil, crayons, for drawing pictures of children standing or sitting.

    ✐ <u>Teacher's Notes:</u> Discussion on results of activity; open format; Teacher records own results.

Mathematics

7. <u>Sorting and Classifying: Treasure Boxes:</u>

   ⇨　Children sort articles in box according to size, shape, color, etc.

   ☺ <u>Skills:</u> These activities help children to organize objects according to their properties or attributes. Logical thinking, language skills, paying attention to small details, and describing small details are also developed from these activities.

   ✂ <u>Materials To Be Used:</u>　Treasure Boxes.

   ✎ <u>Teacher's Notes:</u>　Discussion on results of activity; open format; Teacher records own results.

Mathematics

8. <u>Sorting and Classifying: Walks:</u>

    ⇨ Group activity. (To be used with 4 and 5 year olds.)
    ⇨ Go for a walk looking for things of a certain attribute, such as color, shape, size, real/man-made, growing/not growing, hard/soft, wet/dry, old/new, etc.;
    ⇨ Talk about the things the class has discovered; and/or,
    ⇨ Draw pictures of the things the class has discovered;
    ⇨ One fun idea is to have one child explain something he saw, and then have the other children try to guess what he is describing.

☺ <u>Skills:</u> Connecting an abstract idea to the real world; Selecting objects with a particular property; Comparing; Making judgements; Stimulating visual imagery; Using all the senses to gain information.

✂ <u>Materials To Be Used:</u>   Materials found on walks; Paper and Crayons.

✎ <u>Teacher's Notes:</u> Discussion on results of activity; open format; Teacher records own results.

Mathematics

9. <u>Counting: Count and Turn:</u>

   ➡ The children stand in a row facing the Teacher. They stamp their feet as they count, throwing their arms up in the air to emphasize the last number in the sequence. The children change directions without losing the beat, counting "one" as they turn:

   One, two, three, fooooooour;
   (turn) one, two, three, fooooooour;
   (turn) one, two,........

   ☺ <u>Skills:</u> These activities give the children an opportunity to develop skill with counting sequence—counting forward and backward. These skills are a remote preparation for number concepts.

   ✂ <u>Materials To Be Used:</u>   None

   ✏ <u>Teacher's Notes:</u> Discussion on results of activity; open format; Teacher records own results.

Mathematics

10. <u>Counting: The Pendulum Game:</u>

   ➪   The children watch the pendulum swinging freely and count along with it. The Teacher stops and restarts the motion at the end of the counting sequence.

   ☺ <u>Skills:</u>   Practicing the counting sequence; Learning one-to-one correspondence; Developing a sense of rhythm.

   ✂ <u>Materials To Be Used:</u>   A weight tied to a length of string.

   Pendulum Swinging

   Example:

   1   2   3

   ✎ <u>Teacher's Notes:</u> Discussion on results of activity; open format; Teacher records own results.

Mathematics

II. <u>Counting: Counting Forward:</u>

⇨ The Order of Number Names:

Sample Assessment Strategy:

Action	Interpretation	Instruction
Teacher: "Elsa, count for me."* Child: "One, two, three, five, two, eleven."	Elsa appears to be secure with the counting order to three.	Play the counting games to four (one number beyond the child" point of difficulty).
Teacher: "Miriam, please count for me." Child: "One, two, three, four, five, six, nine, eleven, ten."	Miriam appears to be secure with the counting order to six.	Play the counting games to seven (One number beyond the child's point of difficulty.
Teacher: "Jacob, will you please count for me?" Child: "One, two, three, four, five, six, seven, eight, nine, ten, eleven, twelve, thirteen, fourteen, fifteen, sixteen,...."	Jacob appears to be secure with the counting order to ten and above.	Assess one-to-one correspondence.

*By leaving this question open, rather than suggesting the child count to ten, the child will count as far as she/he is capable.

One-To-One Correspondence:

Action	Interpretation	IInstruction
Teacher: "James, can you find out how many buttons there are in one of these piles?" Child: (James counts the pile with three buttons) "One, two, three."	James appears to have 1:1 correspondence with three objects.	Check further.

Mathematics

12. <u>Counting: Counting Forward (Continued)</u>:

Teacher: "Try another pile." Child: (James counts the pile with seven buttons) "One, two, three, four, five, six."	James appears not to have 1:1 correspondence with seven objects.	Direct the child to count the group of five buttons. (When a child has difficulty, always try a lower number.
Teacher: "James, count this pile of buttons, please." Child: "One, two, three, four, five."	James appears to have 1:1 correspondence with five objects.	Check for six. If the child has difficulty, begin activities stressing 1:1 correspondence counting to six. If the child does not have difficulty, begin the games counting to seven (the number at which the child needs practice).

☺ <u>Skills</u>: The order of number names.

✂ <u>Materials To Be Used</u>: Beans – large and all the same – for counting.

✎ <u>Teacher's Notes</u>: Discussion on results of activity; open format; Teacher records own results. Presentation can be applied to other activities. Keep written or memory records (tracking) of each child's abilities.

Mathematics

12. <u>Counting: The Piggy Bank Game:</u>

   ⇨ The children practice counting in sequence, 1, 2, 3, 4,...., in order to determine the amount of objects in a group. They are also learning that the group of counted objects does not change when hidden from view.

   The Teacher drops whatever amount of objects is appropriate for group of children through a slit in the milk carton or box as the children count out loud. Ask the children to whisper in your ear and tell you how many objects they think there will be when you lift the milk carton. Lift the carton and count together. This activity should be repeated many times, increasing the total number of objects as the children's skill increases.

   This game is used with 4 and 5 year olds.

☺ <u>Skills:</u> Practicing the counting sequence; Using the counting sequence to determine quantity; Learning invariance of number; Experiencing permanence of objects removed from view.

✂ <u>Materials To Be Used:</u> Milk carton; Small objects for counting.

✎ <u>Teacher's Notes:</u> Discussion on results of activity; open format; Teacher records own results.

Mathematics

13. <u>Writing Numbers: Dotted Numbers:</u>

   ⇨   Writing Dotted Numbers on paper to be traced over. As an individual activity give each child 1 sheet to write on at a time. Make sure child is writing number correctly top to bottom. Can also be used as a group activity to show how, then make extra practice papers available as child requests them. Compile into a booklet for each child.

☺ <u>Skills:</u> Development in hand-eye coordination through writing numbers; Development of concepts of numbers.

✂ <u>Materials To Be Used:</u> Paper with dotted numbers and a pencil or crayon.

✏ <u>Teacher's Notes:</u> Discussion on results of activity; open format; Teacher records own results.

Mathematics

14. <u>Writing Numbers: Sandbox and Cards:</u>

   ⇨ Put a small amount of sand in a shallow box, or lid of a box about the size of a shoe box. Make a set of flash cards with the numbers 1-10. Child takes sand box and cards to a table;; places cards next to box in a pile, starting with number 1. Child traces number into sand with pointer finger. Then child shakes number out of sand and writes next one.

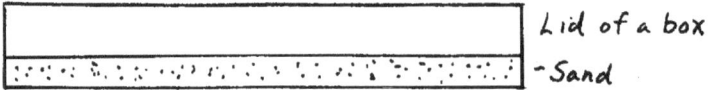

<u>Memo</u>: Draw a happy face in upper right corner so child knows how card faces. Happy face is at the "top" of the card.

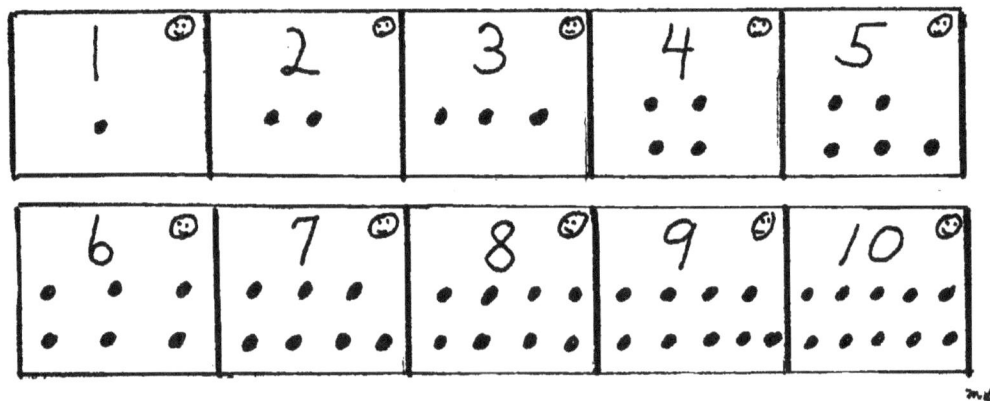

<u>Flash Cards</u>: Each number card should be made separately. Explain to the child how to count the dots...the dots tell what the number is. Also tell the child that the Happy Face is at the top of the card.

☺ <u>Skills</u>: Remote Preparation for Writing; Hand-eye Coordination; Practice Sequencing of Numbers; Small Muscular Control.

✂ <u>Materials To Be Used</u>: Small Box; Sand; Flash Cards; Pencil or Crayon.

✏ <u>Teacher's Notes</u>: Discussion on results of activity; open format; Teacher records own results.

Part 5
♪ Music ♪

Music

In Music we Sing,
    And we listen
        To Sound,
            And we learn
                To express ourselves
                    Dancing around;

Then the instruments help us
    And others join in
        So we learn
           To write Scales;
              Now the fun
                  Can begin!!!

Vanessa Conaway Pace

Introduction To Music

Every race of men, every culture, has discovered how to sing and dance. Music seems to be as natural to the human mind as communication by means of language or the use of tools and inventions to improve the standard of living.

And just as throughout our history languages have become more elaborate and material conditions more comfortable, music has developed from the rhythm of the drum, or a few notes on a whistle, to the complicated orchestrations of today. In fact, ballet, opera, and symphony concerts need performers who have spent years of hard work in training, and even the audience must consist of people who have special musical gifts or education to enable them to appreciate the performance.

There is a tendency, therefore, to think of simple music, or the performances of amateurs, as hardly worthwhile. Sadly, many children become discouraged in their musical education, and give up hope of *understanding*, let alone *producing* music. It is the same process that results in many children losing all interest in reading, and nearly all children thinking that they are quite incapable of arithmetic. This is due simply to the *method of teaching*, not to what is taught.

In some countries where there is less school teaching, and old traditions survive, everyone joins in the singing and dancing, and people do not stop to think whether or not they are "musical". That is a far better state of affairs, for the *need* for music is even older and deeper than the need for other forms of culture. In industrialized civilizations an industry has grown up to supply this deeply felt need for music, but it does not seem that passive listening can properly satisfy the need. There must also be *understanding* and *participation* in making music.

In order that people may grow up with their musical gifts properly developed we must find a way of teaching that does not cause misunderstanding and discouragement, for there is nothing in which special aptitudes vary more widely between one person and another than in musical ability.

Introduction To Music (Continued)

Music must begin early in life. It should play a large part in the preschool curriculum. Listening to music, singing music, dancing to music, and learning about musical instruments and written music are just a few areas that should be offered. All these music areas are interesting and fascinating for the children when presented in a way that allows them to be free and active. It is quite possible for them to get a real knowledge and understanding of the elements of music at an early age, when it is usually thought impossible to teach them anything but a few songs by continual repetition.

The reason we take such care to give children understanding and appreciation of music is not that we wish them to grow up with accomplishments that will enable them to perform and be admired (although that could happen!). It is because a love for music is vital to development. Men have realized the beauty of sounds and used them to develop a new kind of language that gives expression to feelings far more clearly than words. But passive listening is not enough. Music can be sung, played, or expressed in dancing, which has always been important in the emotional and religious life of people. Children should be given this opportunity. At the same time they gradually learn to understand the music and respond to the mood expressed. This is a help to their "harmonious" development.

Remember that Singing, and Movement, and Rhythm Instruments can be combined at any given time in your Preschool Music Activities!

We encourage a lot of music activities in your preschooler's life.

Music

Singing   Dancing   Listening

Skills To Develop

- Vocabulary
- Listening to Sounds

- Memory
- Rhythm

- Music Instruments
- Listening and Recognizing Sounds of Musical Instruments
- Reading Music

Activities – Overview

Singing Songs
Awareness of sound;
- Music Sounds – variety
- Nature Sounds – wind, rain
- Whisper Game
- Echo Clapping

Learning melodies, words and dances
Movement to different types of music and dance;
Jars and Rhythm Sticks
Balance and Coordination
- Walking on a line
- Bell Game

Pictures in "My Music Book of the Orchestra"

Staffs and Notes

Equipment:

Phonograph or Tape Recorder
Records and Tapes
Song Book
Musical Instruments: Rhythm Sticks; Scratchers; Drums

Objectives:

- Love of music. It is important to physical, mental, and emotional development;
- Expressing feelings. Music helps.
- Developing body coordination;
- Developing not only the cultural life, but also the religious life of a people through singing, dancing, and rhythm.

Ideas for Room Arrangement: Music

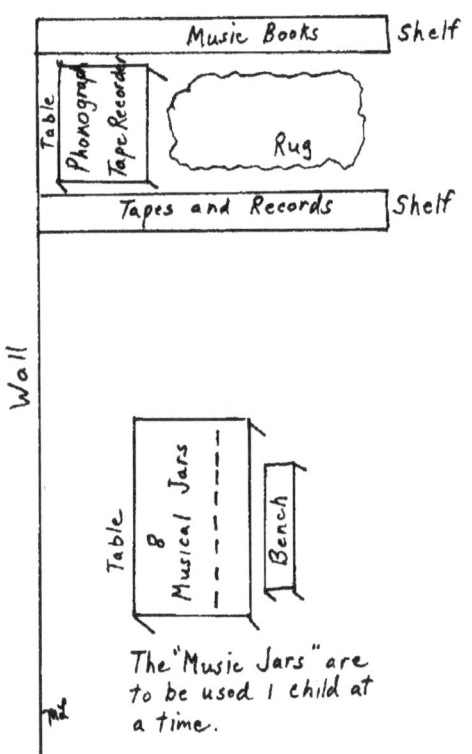

These Music Areas should be located in a comparatively quiet area of the room.

The "Music Jars" are to be used 1 child at a time.

More Activities:

- Marching to record or taped music while playing Rhythm Sticks and Drums;
- Walking and Clicking Game:
  - The children learn to click Rhythm Sticks as they walk fast or slow (No music);
  - The children learn to hit Rhythm Sticks softly when walking softly, and loudly when walking (stomping) loudly.
- Sound and Silence:
  - The children listen for sounds and silence;
  - They move when there is sound (music), and stand still when there is silence.

More Activities: Music (Continued):

- Chanting Game
    - The children participate in a "singing dialogue", rather than a "spoken dialogue";
    - They sing or chant responses to statements sung to them by the adult.

Example 1:

Teacher/Caregiver:	Chant line:	___	___	___	___	___
	Words:	"Good	morn -	ing	child -	ren."

Children:	Chant line:	___	___	___	___	___
	Words:	"Good	morn -	ing	Teach -	er."

Example 2:

Teacher/Caregiver:	Chant line:	___	___	___	___	___	___
	Words:	"It	is	now	time	for	lunch."

Children:	Chant line:	___	___	___	___	___	___
	Words:	"It	is	now	time	for	lunch."

Music Through Movement

1. <u>Sound Walk:</u> Children go on a "Sound Walk". Children sit in an outside area and listen for sounds around them. What do you hear? Discuss. Children may walk and stop in different areas – listen – discuss what they hear.

    ☺ <u>Skills:</u> Listed at front of Music Section.

    ✂ <u>Materials To Be Used:</u> None

    ✎ <u>Teacher's Notes:</u> Discussion on results of activity; open format; Teacher records own results.

Music Through Movement

2. <u>Sounds Inside:</u> Children sit in a circle - close eyes. Teacher makes a sound (tap a pencil, snap fingers, ring a small bell, etc.), then ask children what they heard.

☺ <u>Skills:</u> Listed at front of Music Section.

✂ <u>Materials To Be Used:</u> Small objects for making sounds.

✐ <u>Teacher's Notes:</u> Discussion on results of activity; open format; Teacher records own results.

Music Through Movement

3. <u>Body Sounds:</u> Children sit in circle on floor. Tell them they can make their own sounds with their bodies.

    ➪ Clap hands: Make different patterns;
    ➪ Tap feet on floor: Make different patterns;
    ➪ Hum with lips closed: Make up sounds; Soft/Loud;
    ➪ Sing: Sing a simple melody or song.

☺ <u>Skills:</u> Listed at front of Music Section.

✄ <u>Materials To Be Used:</u> Our bodies; Imagination!

✐ <u>Teacher's Notes:</u> Discussion on results of activity; open format; Teacher records own results.

Music Through Movement

4. <u>Music in the Dance:</u> Children in circle on floor. Tell them they can make their own music through dance.

    ⇨ Game: "Color Dancing": We can put music with this movement to make dance - all kinds of dance:

        ⇨ Exercise: If you were the color yellow how would you move? (Yellow may be more gentle and flowing - slow dance);
        ⇨ Exercise: If you were the color red how would you move? (Red may be described as an explosion with high jumps.)

☺ <u>Skills:</u> Listed at front of Music Section.

✂ <u>Materials To Be Used:</u> Our bodies; Imagination!

✏ <u>Teacher's Notes:</u> Discussion on results of activity; open format; Teacher records own results.

Music Through Movement

5. <u>Circle Game:</u>

    ⇨ Play music with rhythm instrument, like drum, or records or tapes;
    ⇨ The children interpret the music played in movement.

☺ <u>Skills:</u> Listed at front of Music Section.

✂ <u>Materials To Be Used:</u>   Our bodies; Rhythm instruments; Records or tapes; Imagination!

✎ <u>Teacher's Notes:</u> Discussion on results of activity; open format; Teacher records own results.

Music Through Movement

6. <u>Move on the Beat:</u>

    ⇨ Jump on each clap or drum beat;
    ⇨ Hop on each clap or drum beat;
    ⇨ March on each clap or drum beat.

☺ <u>Skills:</u> Listed at front of Music Section.

✂ <u>Materials To Be Used:</u> Our bodies; Rhythm instruments; Records or tapes; Imagination!

✎ <u>Teacher's Notes:</u> Discussion on results of activity; open format; Teacher records own results.

Music Through Movement

7. <u>Bell Game:</u>

    ⇨ Teacher brings a small bell to Gathering/Circle Time;

    ⇨ She shows the bell to the children, and then places it on the floor in front of her;

    ⇨ She explains that she is going to pick up the bell slowly and try to walk carefully all around the circle without the bell ringing;

    ⇨ If the bell rings while she is walking she will place the bell down in front of that child;

    ⇨ That boy or girl will then pick up the bell and try to go all the way around the circle;

    ⇨ If he or she makes it all the way around they may choose who they want to have the bell next.

☺ <u>Skills:</u> Listed at front of Music Section.

✂ <u>Materials To Be Used:</u> A bell with a handle.

✎ <u>Teacher's Notes:</u> Discussion on results of activity; open format; Teacher records own results.

Music Through Movement

8. <u>Whisper Game:</u>

    ⇨ Children are sitting quietly;

    ⇨ One child goes to the other side of the room – out of sight – and whispers another child's name;

    ⇨ The Whisper Game can go until the Teacher feels that enough children have participated.

☺ <u>Skills:</u> Listed at front of Music Section.

✄ <u>Materials To Be Used:</u> None.

✎ <u>Teacher's Notes:</u> Discussion on results of activity; open format; Teacher records own results.

Music Through Movement

9. <u>Walking a Line Game:</u>

   ⇨　A 6-8 foot string is placed on the ground;
   ⇨　The children take turns seeing how far they can walk on the string.

☺ <u>Skills:</u> Listed at front of Music Section.

✂ <u>Materials To Be Used:</u>

✐ <u>Teacher's Notes:</u> Discussion on results of activity; open format; Teacher records own results.

Music Through Movement

10. <u>Weather Music:</u> Reproduce weather sounds while making up movements:

    ⇨   Rain: Strike 2 wooden sticks with quick motions;
    ⇨   Wind: Child makes blowing wind sound while dancing like the wind;
    ⇨   Thunder: Child dances and claps loudly;
    ⇨   Others in circle can also make sounds while one or two children do the dance.

☺ <u>Skills:</u> Listed at front of Music Section.

✄ <u>Materials To Be Used:</u> Sticks; Children's own sounds.

✎ <u>Teacher's Notes:</u> Discussion on results of activity; open format; Teacher records own results.

Music Through Singing

Row, Row, Row Your Boat

Round

Row, row, row your boat gent-ly down the stream,

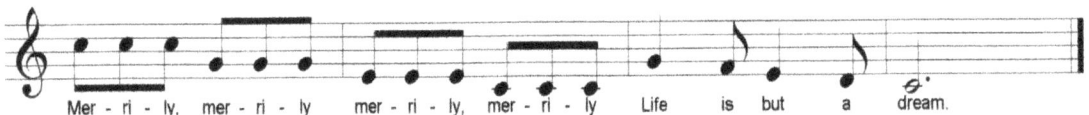
Mer-ri-ly, mer-ri-ly, mer-ri-ly, mer-ri-ly Life is but a dream.

☺ <u>Skills:</u> Singing, Rhythm, Movement, Co-ordination, Expression, Exercise

♪ <u>Movement While Singing:</u> Children pretend they are sitting in a boat rowing. Repeat song three times – singing and rowing a little faster each time.

📖 <u>Extension Of Ideas:</u> Gather pictures and items that share ideas about different kinds of sea life, bodies of water, fish, boats, etc.

✏ <u>Teacher's Notes:</u>

Music Through Singing

Are You Sleeping

Round

☺ **Skills:** Singing, Rhythm, Movement, Co-ordination, Expression, Exercise

♪ **Movement While Singing:** First line of song: children sing softly; Second line of song: children sing with normal voice. Repeat the song in French. The last verse ("Where is (Name Child.)?") is a separate activity. The children sing this greeting to welcome each other during Circle Time at the beginning of the day.

📖 **Extension Of Ideas:** Talk about the different types of sound (soft and loud), and how our voices, things around us or in Nature, and things we handle, can make different sounds. (Example: Hitting two sticks together can be done loudly or softly.) Practice "listening" to different sounds in music and Nature.

✎ **Teacher's Notes:**

Music Through Singing

Bingo

Scotland

There was a farmer had a dog. And Bin-go was his name, O,
B - I - N - G - O, B - I - N - G - O, B - I - N - G - O, And Bin-go was his name, - O.

There was a farmer had a cat. And Jin-go was her name, O,
J - I - N - G - O, J - I - N - G - O, J - I - N - G - O, And Jin-go was her name, - O.

☺ <u>Skills:</u> Singing, Rhythm, Movement, Co-ordination, Expression, Exercise

♪ <u>Movement While Singing:</u> Children clap hands while singing and spelling "B - I - N - G - O". Children clap hands while singing and spelling "J - I - N - G - O".

📖 <u>Extension Of Ideas:</u> Talk about the different aspects of outdoor life. Suggestion: Make pictures and examples of animals, plant life, terrain, etc., available for the children to talk about.

✎ <u>Teacher's Notes:</u>

Music Through Singing

He's Got the Whole World in His Hands

Spiritual

- 😊 <u>Skills:</u> Singing, Rhythm, Movement, Co-ordination, Expression, Exercise

- 🎵 <u>Movement While Singing:</u> Children stand and act out the words of the song while singing each verse.

- 📖 <u>Extension Of Ideas:</u> Show maps and talk about the different continents and the different cultures of people around the world.

- ✏ <u>Teacher's Notes:</u>

Music Through Singing

Go In and Out the Window

United States of America

Go in and out the win-dow, Go in and out the win-dow. Go
Go forth and choose your part-ner. Go forth and choose your part-ner. Go
Go un-der-neath the ar-ches. Go un-der-neath the ar-ches. Go

in and out the win - dow, As we have done be - fore. love.
forth and choose your part - ner, As we have done be - fore.
un - der - neath the ar - ches, As we have done be - fore.

- ☺ <u>Skills:</u> Singing, Rhythm, Movement, Co-ordination, Expression, Exercise

- ♫ <u>Movement While Singing:</u> Verse 1: All children stand, join hands, and raise hands up while standing in a circle. One child walks in and out under the arches created by the raised arms and joined hands of the circled children. Verses 2 and 3: That child chooses a partner to walk in and out under the arches with him/her. The song can be repeated choosing a new child for the activity.

- 📖 <u>Extension Of Ideas:</u> Discuss how we might share space, things, etc., with others/partners.

- ✎ <u>Teacher's Notes:</u>

Music Through Singing

Oh Where, Oh Where Has My Little Dog Gone?

German Folk Song

Oh where, oh where has my lit-tle dog gone? Oh where, oh where can he be? With his tail cut short and his ears cut long. Oh where, oh where can he be?

Oh where, oh where has my lit-tle dog gone? Oh where, oh where can he be? I will look for him, and will call for him. And he will come back to me!!!

☺ <u>Skills:</u> Singing, Rhythm, Movement, Co-ordination, Expression, Exercise

♪ <u>Movement While Singing:</u> Children stand in a circle pretending to look around for their lost animal.

📖 <u>Extension Of Ideas:</u> Talk about pets. Share pictures and stories about pets. Have the children talk about what animal they would like to have for a pet. No limits on the imagination!! Go creative!!!

✒ <u>Teacher's Notes:</u>

Music Through Singing

The More We Get Together

Germany

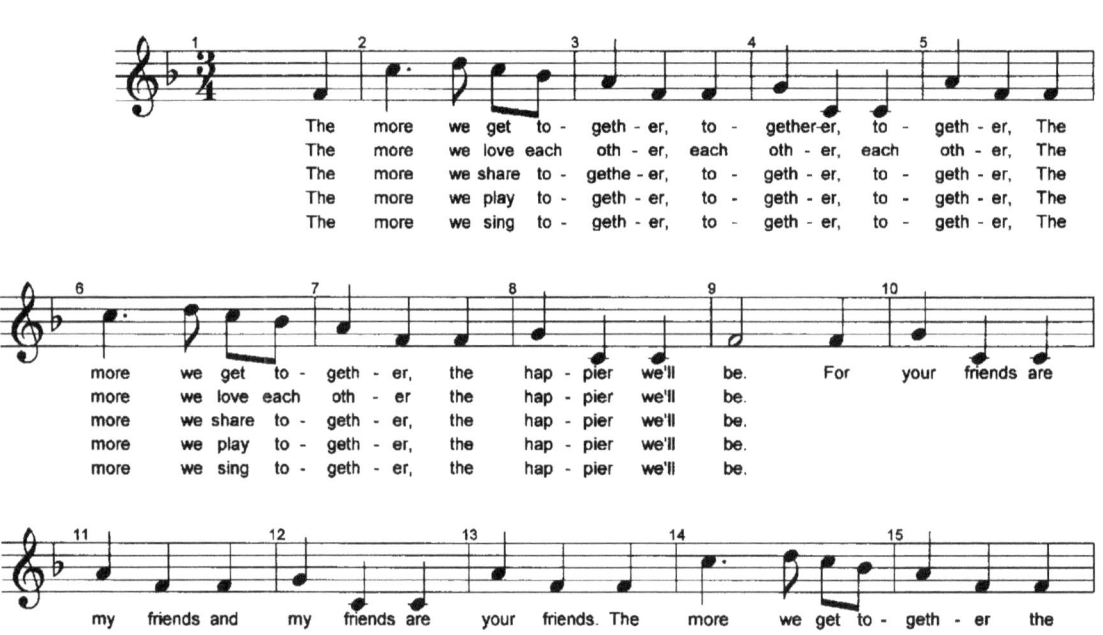

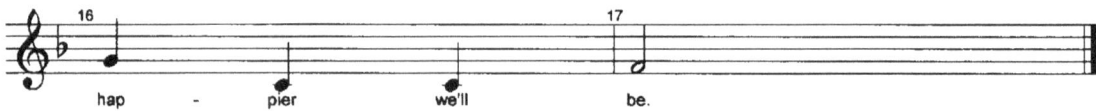

☺ <u>Skills:</u> Singing, Rhythm, Movement, Co-ordination, Expression, Exercise

♪ <u>Movement While Singing:</u> During the Chorus the children turn and point to each other (For your friends are my friends, etc.).

📖 <u>Extension Of Ideas:</u> Discuss what a friend is; how we make friends; who our friends are; and what we do with our friends. Let the children talk about their experiences with their friends.

✏ <u>Teacher's Notes:</u>

Music Through Singing

Kum Ba Yah
(Come By Here)

African Hymn

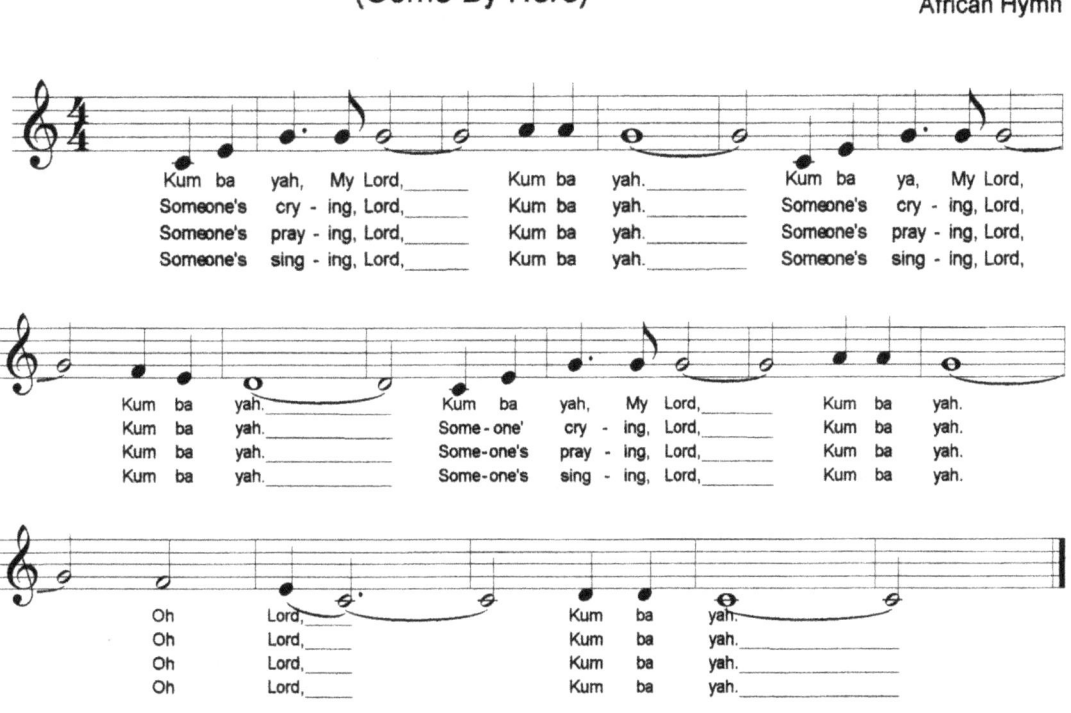

☺ <u>Skills:</u> Singing, Rhythm, Movement, Co-ordination, Expression, Exercise

♪ <u>Movement While Singing:</u> The children stand, sway a little back and forth, and act out the verses. Free expression.

📖 <u>Extension Of Ideas:</u> Share how we can help each other to feel good, be happy, and lead good lives.

✎ <u>Teacher's Notes:</u>

Music Through Singing

The Mulberry Bush

English Country Dance Tune

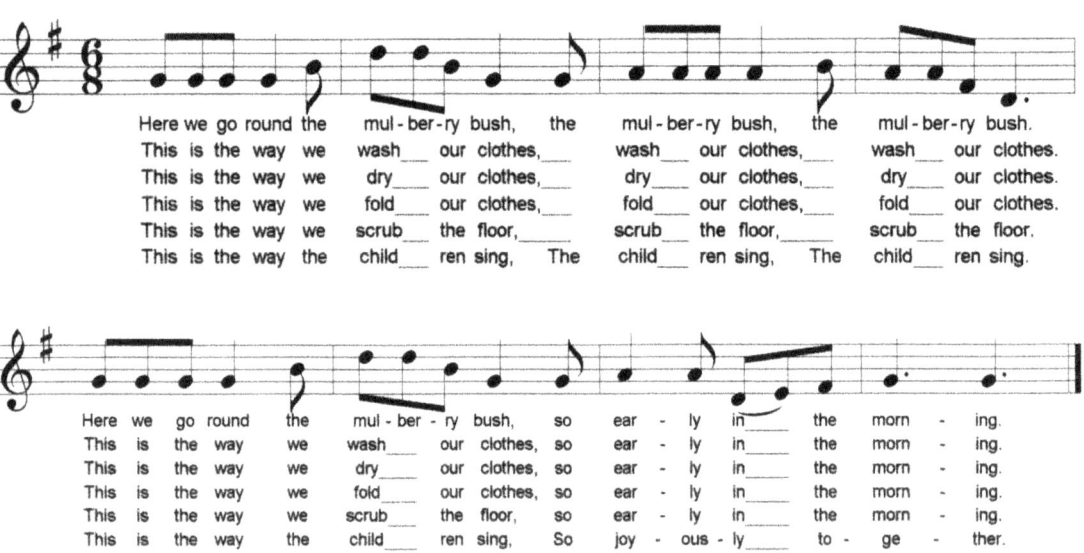

Here we go round the mul-ber-ry bush, the mul-ber-ry bush, the mul-ber-ry bush.
This is the way we wash our clothes, wash our clothes, wash our clothes.
This is the way we dry our clothes, dry our clothes, dry our clothes.
This is the way we fold our clothes, fold our clothes, fold our clothes.
This is the way we scrub the floor, scrub the floor, scrub the floor.
This is the way the child-ren sing, The child-ren sing, The child-ren sing.

Here we go round the mul-ber-ry bush, so ear-ly in the morn-ing.
This is the way we wash our clothes, so ear-ly in the morn-ing.
This is the way we dry our clothes, so ear-ly in the morn-ing.
This is the way we fold our clothes, so ear-ly in the morn-ing.
This is the way we scrub the floor, so ear-ly in the morn-ing.
This is the way the child-ren sing, So joy-ous-ly to-ge-ther.

☺ <u>Skills:</u> Singing, Rhythm, Movement, Co-ordination, Expression, Exercise

♫ <u>Movement While Singing:</u> Verse 1: The children stand and clap in rhythm while walking around the room. In the rest of the verses the children stand, sing, and do the appropriate actions.

📖 <u>Extension Of Ideas:</u> Discuss how we can be helpful with chores at school and at home.

✏ <u>Teacher's Notes:</u>

Music Through Singing

Eency, Weency Spider

Action Song

Een-cy, ween-cy spi-der went up the wa-ter spout;
Down came the rain and washed the spi-der out;
Out came the sun and dried up all the rain, And the
een-cy ween-cy spi-der went up the spout a-gain.

☺ <u>Skills:</u> Singing, Rhythm, Movement, Co-ordination, Expression, Exercise

♪ <u>Movement While Singing:</u> Line 1: Children wiggle fingers like a spider, raising arms up. Line 2: Arms come back down to show the rain coming down and washing the spider out. Line 3: Children's arms go up above their heads forming a ball like the sun. Line 4: Arms come back down and the children raise them up again while wiggling their fingers like a spider.

📖 <u>Extension Of Ideas:</u> Talk about insects, and where they live, etc. Show pictures and examples of insects.

✎ <u>Teacher's Notes:</u>

Children's Music Book of the Orchestra

<u>Presentation Instructions:</u>

- ⇨ Take each section of the Orchestra and talk about it as the children look at that particular section. For example: The String Section.
- ⇨ If possible have a record or tape of string instrument music.
- ⇨ Then let the children color in those sections of the Orchestra involving string instruments.
- ⇨ Then let the children color in the pictures of the string instruments.
- ⇨ Collect the children's booklets and keep them until the next music session.
- ⇨ Then, review the previous lesson, and move on to the next section of the Orchestra – String Instruments – Woodwind Instruments – Brass Instruments – Percussion Instruments.
- ⇨ When each child's "My Music Book of the Orchestra" has been completed they may take it home.

☺ <u>Skills:</u> Listed at front of Music Section.

✂ <u>Materials To Be Used:</u> Listening Tapes or Records; Children's Own Music Book.

✎ <u>Teacher's Notes:</u> Discussion on results of activity; open format; Teacher records own results.

My Music Book Of the Orchestra

My Music Book of the Orchestra

Music makes the world go round
    And everything that's in it.

    Its study
        Will reveal its truths
            If you
                Will just
                    Begin it!

You'll learn
    About the Orchestra
        And Instruments within it;

        And learn
            To write the music down
                For others
                    In a minute!

Wow!
    Just like You,
        Each Instrument
            Has its own
                Unique sound,

Which keeps
    The whole world singing
        With Sound
            That does
                Abound!!

Vanessa Conaway Pace

THE ORCHESTRA

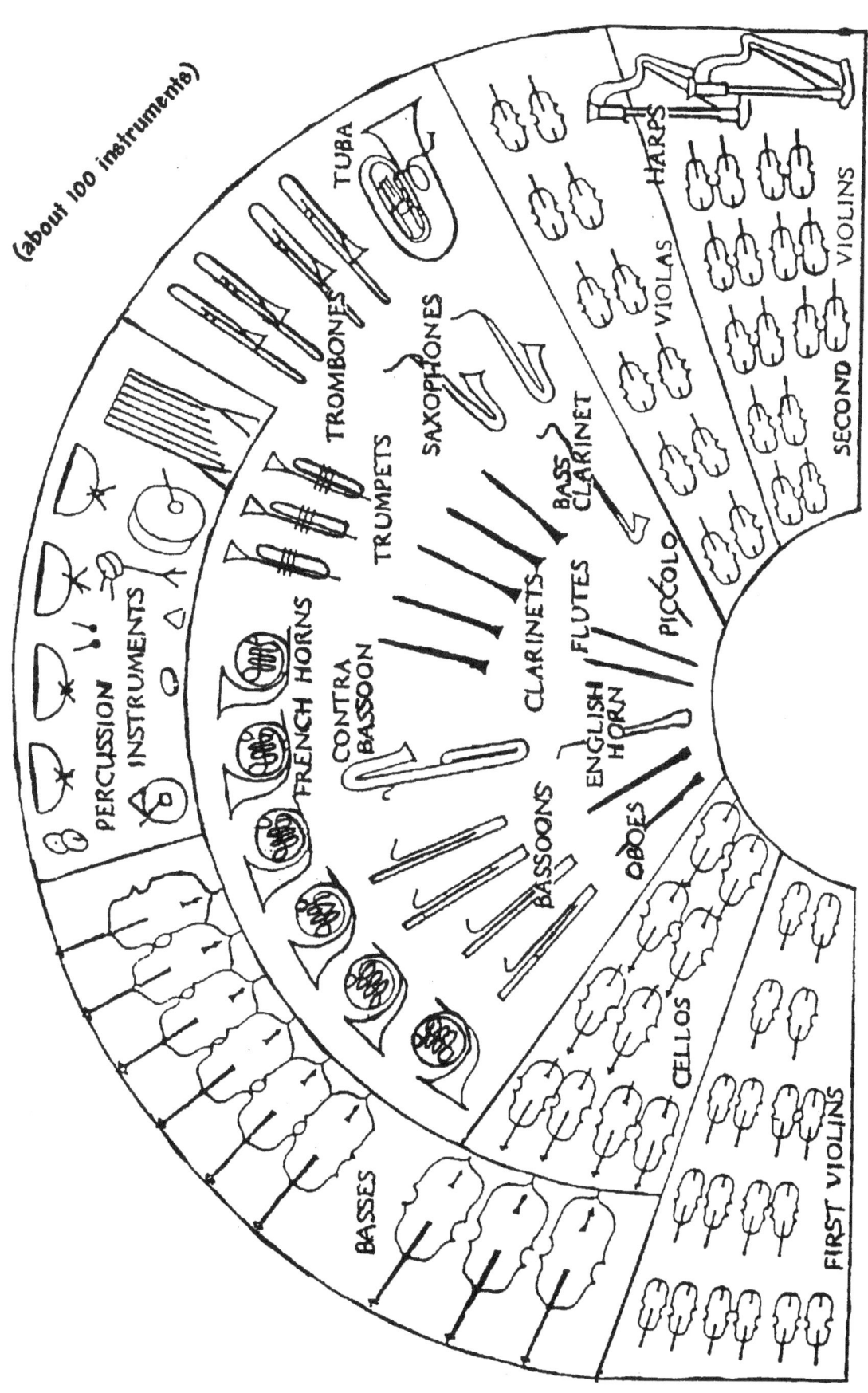

THE ORCHESTRA (Continued)

The Conductor

INSTRUMENTS OF THE ORCHESTRA

THE STRING INSTRUMENTS

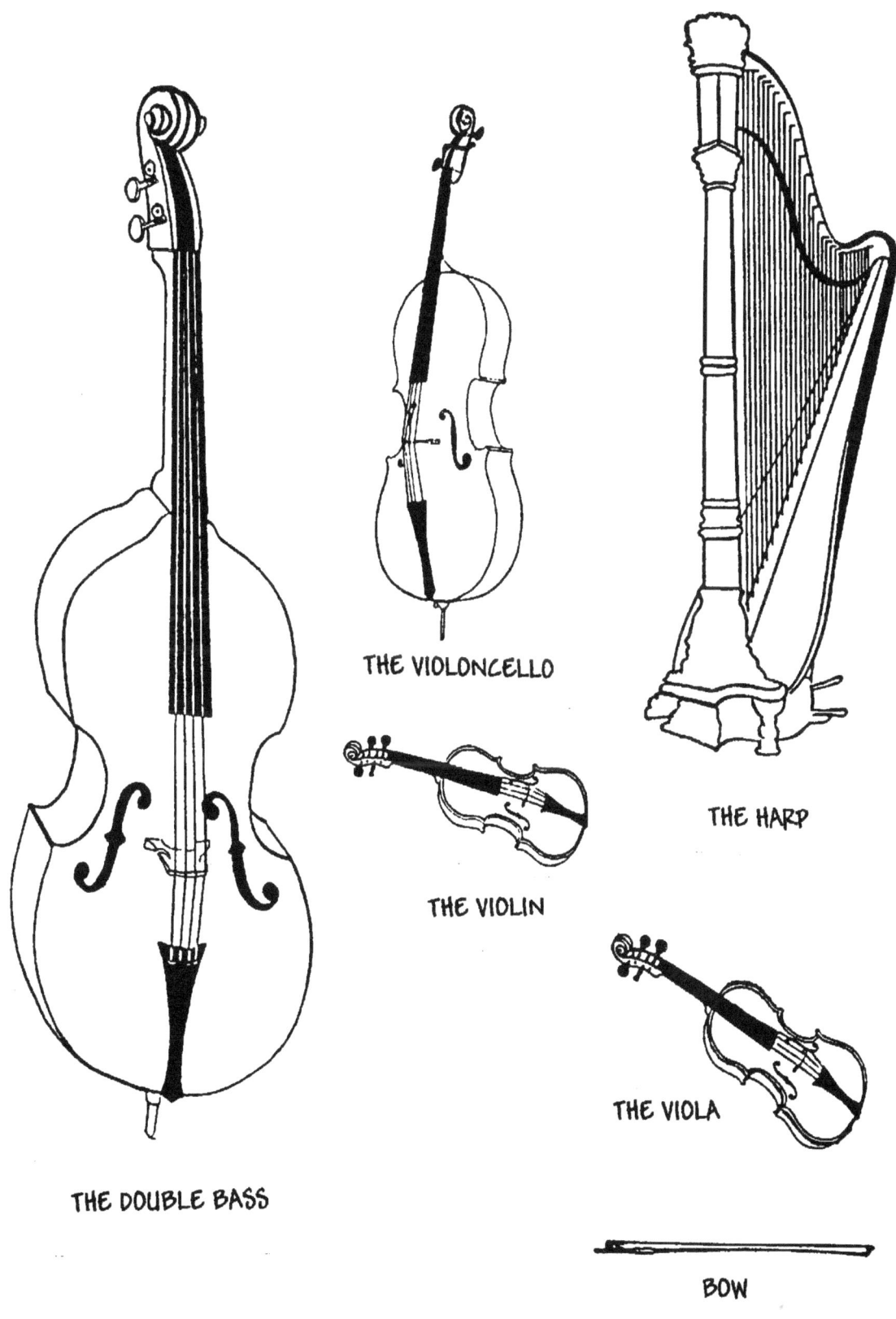

INSTRUMENTS OF THE ORCHESTRA (Continued)

THE WOODWIND INSTRUMENTS

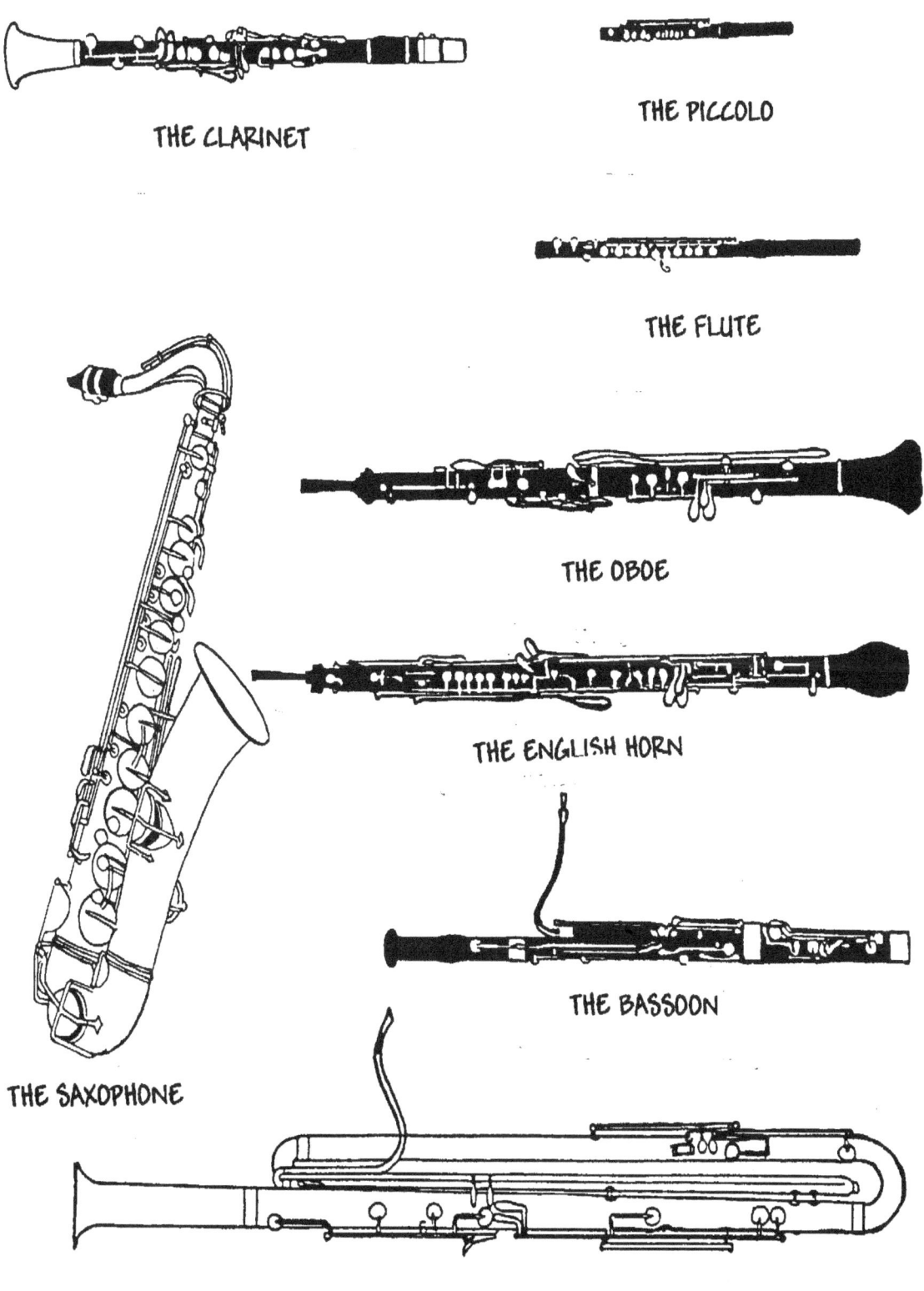

www.fortheloveofchildrenbook.com   E-mail: info@.fortheloveofchildrenbook.com

INSTRUMENTS OF THE ORCHESTRA (Continued)

THE BRASS INSTRUMENTS

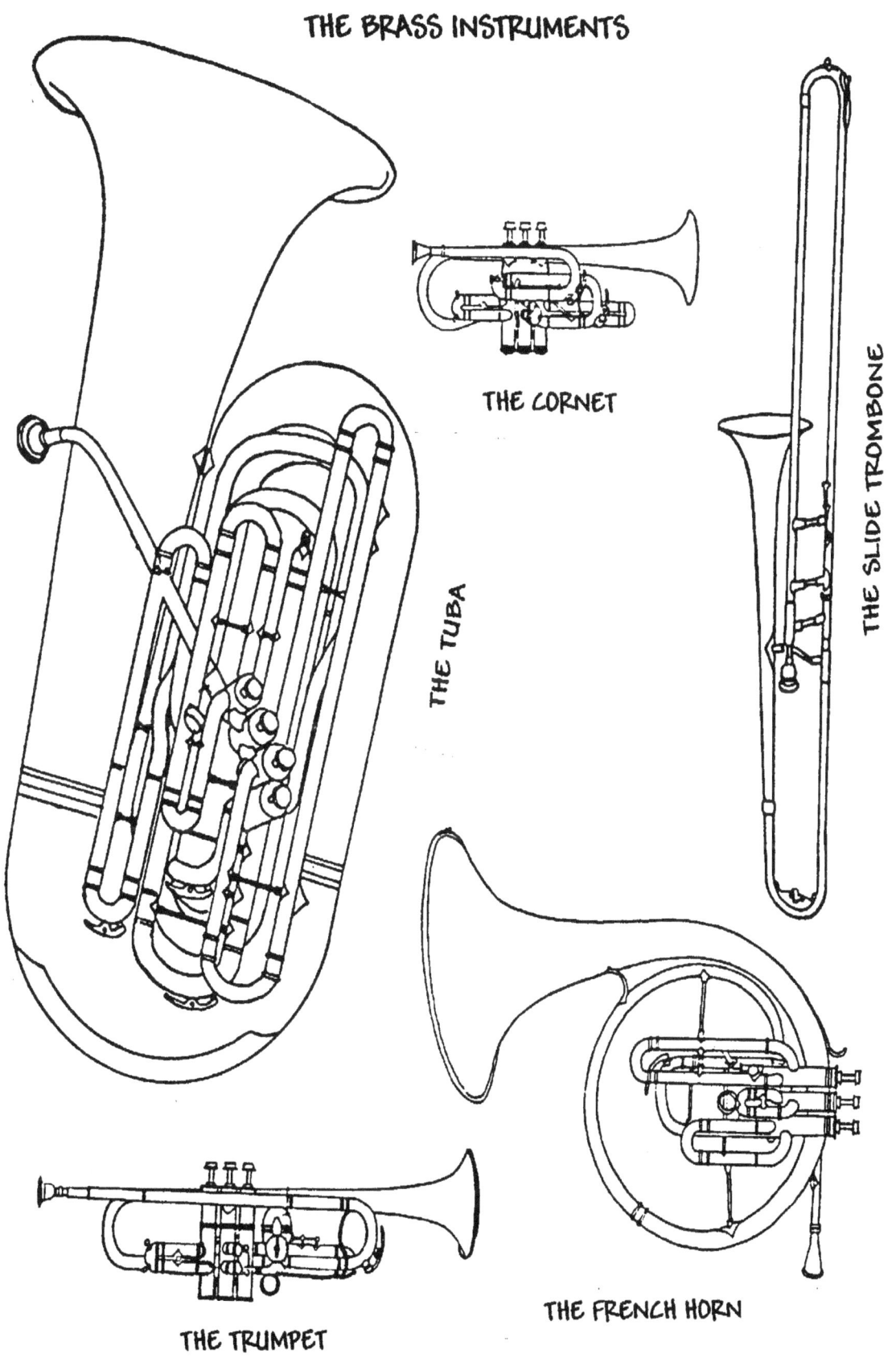

www.fortheloveofchildrenbook.com   E-mail: info@.fortheloveofchildrenbook.com

INSTRUMENTS OF THE ORCHESTRA (Continued)

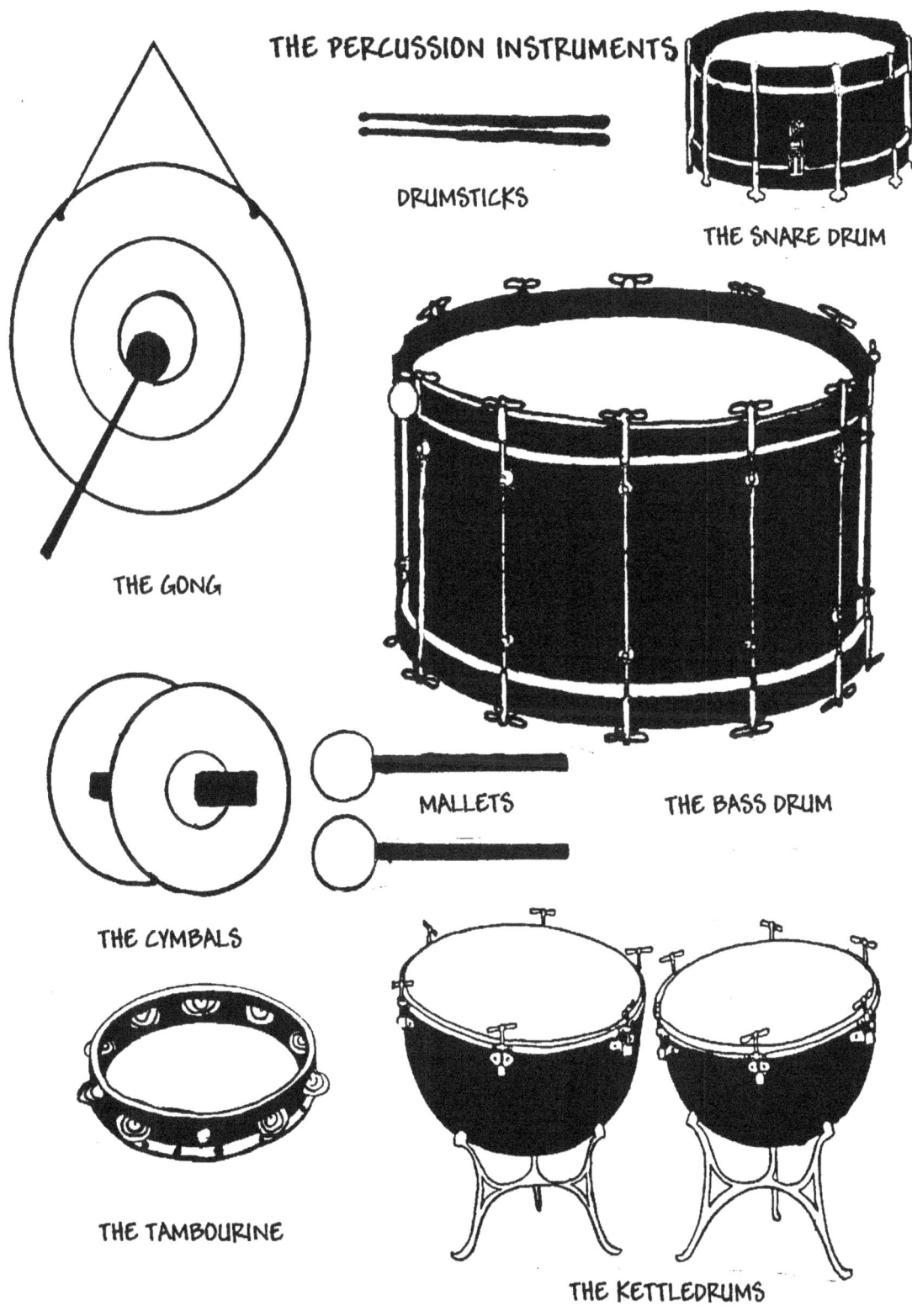

183

www.fortheloveofchildrenbook.com   E-mail: info@.fortheloveofchildrenbook.com

INSTRUMENTS OF THE ORCHESTRA (Continued)

THE PERCUSSION INSTRUMENTS (Continued)

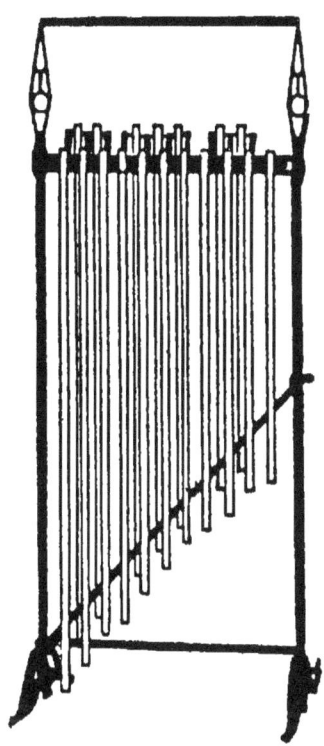

THE CHIMES

THE TRIANGLE

THE CASTANETS

THE XYLOPHONE

THE CELESTA

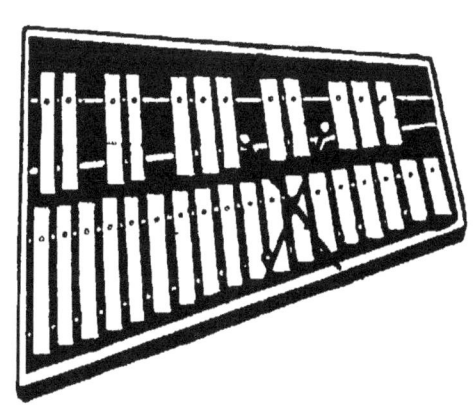

THE GLOCKENSPIEL

Music Instruments – Listening and Playing Jars

1. **Lesson A: Presenting One Jar and Striker:**

   The Teacher takes one jar and the striker to Gathering/Circle Time. Placing the jar on a small table, she shows the child how to strike gently the side of the jar. She listens to the note dying away. She repeats this once or twice. Each time she strikes the jar she sings the note. She shows the child how to stop the sound when he wants to by putting a finger gently on the jar. Each child should have a turn striking the jar. He listens and may try to sing the note (if he does not want to sing do not force it). Let the children have the experience of listening to a single note.

2. **Lesson B: The Octave: (The child has had Lesson A)**

   The Teacher places 2 jars – Middle C and the High (Octave) C on a small table. She strikes Middle C, then the High (Octave) C. These 2 jars are the same pitch, one octave (8 notes) apart. Let each child have a turn playing and listening as in Lesson A..

   While the Teacher is playing the Middle C jar, she adds the activity of having the children bending very low for Middle C, and standing on their toes stretching up high when she plays the High (Octave) C.

3. **Lesson C: The Scale:**

   The Teacher reviews Lesson B, then sets up all 8 jars at a table. She shows the children how to play them, letting each child play them and listen to the sounds.

4. **The Scale in Motion:**

   The Teacher reviews Lesson C of playing all 8 jars. Then she has the children bending low down and standing up gradually as she plays the jars from Middle C up to the High (Octave) C, where the child is stretching as high as possible.

Music Instruments – Listening and Playing Jars

5. <u>Making Music:</u>

The Teacher shows the children how to sit at a table where the 8 jars are lined up in order. She shows them how to play the jars. Then one child at a time may sit – alone – and quietly "play" the jars with the striker. They need not play jars in order, but can make up their own "music". Jars should not be moved around. When the child is finished playing his or her music, he or she leaves the striker on the table with the jars, and leaves the "music" table. Then another child may have a turn.

☺ <u>Skills:</u> Listed at front of Music Section.

✂ <u>Materials To Be Used:</u> Eight jars with water in them. The water level increases as the jar sound corresponds to the white notes on the piano between middle C and high C.

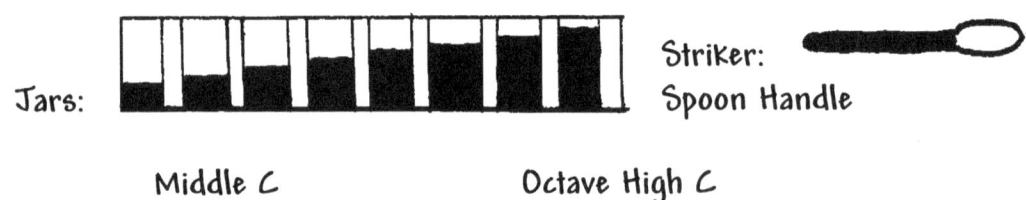

Jars: Striker: Spoon Handle

Middle C   Octave High C

✎ <u>Teacher's Notes:</u> Discussion on results of activity; open format; Teacher records own results.

Reading Music

The Teacher Presents the Musical Staff in Circle Time:

1. <u>First Lesson: The Staff:</u> The Teacher brings only one Staff to the Circle; shows the children the Staff; and tells them that the Staff is:

    ⇨ Used to write music on so people can read the music and sing it and play it on their musical instruments (show the children a sample from the Music Section);

    ⇨ Made with lines and spaces. (Teacher lets the children come up to her large staff and point to the "lines" and "spaces".)

2. <u>Second Lesson: The Note:</u> During Gathering Time – Circle Time give each child their own "staff".

    ⇨ Review the First Lesson, letting each child point to the "lines" and "spaces" on their own "staff";

    ⇨ Then present the musical note;

    ⇨ Tell the children that the "note" is used on the staff in order to write a song;

    ⇨ Give each child a "note";

    ⇨ Show the children how to place the "note" on a line and on a space.

    ⇨ Then show the child how to start the note on "Middle C" and move it up the staff – line to space to line – until it reaches the top of the staff.

    ⇨ Then have them come down the staff.

    ⇨ Collect the "notes" in a cup;

    ⇨ Collect the staffs.

3. <u>Third Lesson: Playing the Sounds:</u> Repeat Lesson 2, and as the children start the "note" on "Middle C", play the jars starting with the first – Low Middle C – and, as the "note" goes up – line to space – play the coinciding jar – From Low (Middle) C to "High (Octave) C".

At this point the 8 jars and the striker should be placed on a table with a staff and note. One child at a time should be able to go to the table as they want to and play the jars and work with the staff and note also.

The above lessons should be reviewed many times in a group.

Reading Music

4. <u>Fourth Lesson: Seeing the Patterns:</u> Show the children written music in a music book. Have them point to the "staff" and the "notes". Show them how the "notes" go up and down on the "staff", making music.

5. <u>Fifth Lesson: Listening and Review:</u> Have the children listen to short musical pieces.

   ⇨ Re-introduce "musical instruments" – their sounds;
   ⇨ Re-introduce "Staff" and "Notes", stating again that a person reads these in order to play certain music.

These lessons should be repeated often. Also, it is very important that children be able to listen to good music, and to sing and dance to good music. A classroom music program should include all facets of music.

☺ <u>Skills:</u> Listed at front of Music Section.

✂ <u>Materials To Be Used:</u> 8 Jars (used in previous activities); Small "Staff" for each child

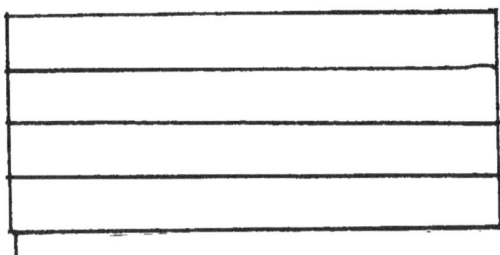

8 Note "Beginning Staff"

The first added line below the staff is Middle C.

(1) Staff made out of heavy cardboard. Straight lines drawn on with heavy black pen or crayon (Size: Large enough for the child to have in front of him on the table or floor. Length: 1 ½ foot by 1 foot, approximately;

(2) Large beans or buttons to be used as musical "notes".

✎ <u>Teacher's Notes:</u> Discussion on results of activity; open format; Teacher records own results.

Introduction To Written Music

Building a Scale on a Staff

Presentation:

1. Set out the board with the C Major scale painted on it:

    ⇨ Identify it;

    ⇨ Sing it by the names of the notes;

    ⇨ Count the notes, and then sing the scale by the numbers of the notes from 1 to 8;

    ⇨ Explain that every scale has eight notes, and that is why it is called an *octave*.

2. Set out the blank board:

    ⇨ Identify it as the musical staff;

    ⇨ Count the five lines;

    ⇨ Count the four intervening spaces;

    ⇨ Call attention to the quarter-line and space at the bottom left;

    ⇨ Explain that there may be many such lines and spaces both below and above the staff.

3. Spread out the wooden discs:

    ⇨ Examine them on both sides;

    ⇨ Turn them number-side up;

    ⇨ Arrange them in a row from 1 to 8;

    ⇨ Turn each one over and point out that the resulting arrangement of note-names matches the order of note-names in the C Major scale on the control board;

    ⇨ Put each note-disc on its proper line or space on the blank musical staff so that you make a C Major scale like the one on the control board;

    ⇨ Sing the scale by note-names.

Introduction To Written Music

Building a Scale on a Staff (Continued)

Note Placement: When the notes are in proper position, the numbers on their reverse side will read in order from 1 to 8.

Age: 4 to 5 years

☺ Skills: To place the lettered note-discs of the C Major scale properly in position on a staff; to prepare for reading music; to coordinate movement.

✂ Materials To Be Used: A wooden board with a musical staff painted on it, and on the staff the notes for the C Major scale. On each note is written the name of that note.

A wooden board with a blank musical staff painted on it, and, at the bottom left, a quarter-line (for middle C). Each line and space may be grooved so that it can hold a wooden note-disc.

Eight black wooden discs, each with the name of one note of the C Major scale on one side, and, on the other, a number from 1 to 8, corresponding to the position of the note in the ascending C Major progression.

Box to hold the discs.

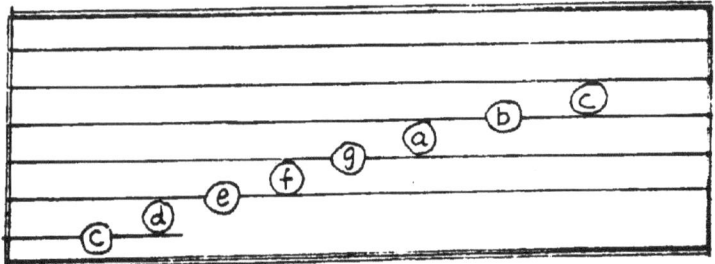

✎ Teacher's Notes: Discussion on results of activity; open format; Teacher records own results.

Matching Game for Naming the Notes Of the C Major Scale

(This is a group game.)

Game:

- ⇨ Stack in order the eight cards that have both note and name on them;
- ⇨ Hold up the Middle C card for the children to see;
- ⇨ Say, "This is Middle C".
- ⇨ Point to the name and repeat it: "Middle C".
- ⇨ Lay the card down so all the children may see it easily;
- ⇨ Present the remaining cards, in order, in the same way. (Later, mix the order.)
- ⇨ Pass out the replica cards and the name cards;
- ⇨ Ask: "Who has Middle C?" (At first, ask for the notes of the scale in order; later, mix the order.)
- ⇨ The child with the replica card of Middle C lays his card down below the Middle C card already there;
- ⇨ Ask: "Who has the name of Middle C?" (Point to the words "Middle C";
- ⇨ The child with the name card for Middle C lays his card just under the replica card, so that now the match for the Middle C card is complete.
- ⇨ Continue in a similar manner with the other cards.
- ⇨ Later, ask each child also to say the name of whatever he is matching.
- ⇨ Encourage the children to play the game on their own.

<u>To insure accuracy:</u>   Child can see whether the configurations of note and staff and name match or not.

<u>Age:</u>   4 to 5 years

Matching Game for Naming the Notes
Of the C Major Scale (Continued)

☺ <u>Skills:</u> To learn the names of the notes of the C Major scale; and to prepare for reading music.

✂ <u>Materials To Be Used:</u> A set of matching cards for all the notes of the C Major scale. For each note there are three cards:

    1.   Replica of note and name of note;
    2.   Replica of note only;
    3.   Name of note only.

Notes are black; cards are white.

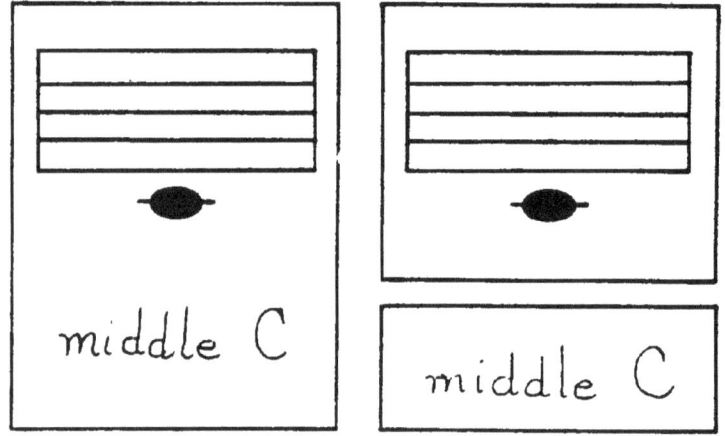

✏ <u>Teacher's Notes:</u> Discussion on results of activity; open format; Teacher records own results.

Making Music with Rhythm Instruments

1. <u>Something To Hit:</u>

   <u>Drums:</u>
   ⇨ Use different size tin cans. Turn them upside down and use pencil or wooden spoon to tap;
   ⇨ Stretch pieces of inner-tube over a coffee can or cereal box, and lace on to make a tom-tom;
   ⇨ Use a block of wood and a wooden clothespin for a beater.

   <u>Cymbals:</u>
   ⇨ Two pan lids.

   <u>Sand Blocks:</u>
   ⇨ Attach sandpaper to two small blocks of wood with glue;

2. <u>Something To Shake:</u>

   ⇨ Place dried beans, peas, rice, or pebbles between two paper plates and staple or sew;
   ⇨ Flatten a toilet paper tube, close one end with tape, fill with beans, etc., and then close the open end. Decorate and shake;
   ⇨ Shake a ring of measuring spoons.

3. <u>Something To Pluck:</u>

   ⇨ Put a rubber band around an empty can;
   ⇨ Put rubber bands around small boxes.

☺ <u>Skills:</u> Listed at front of Music Section.

✂ <u>Materials To Be Used:</u> As listed within each project.

✎ <u>Teacher's Notes:</u> Discussion on results of activity; open format; Teacher records own results.

Music Instruments – Listening and Playing Rhythm Sticks

During Gathering/Circle Time show the children 2 Rhythm Sticks – one held in each hand. Show them how to keep time with music by striking them together. Let the children listen to a record or tape while trying to keep the rhythm by "playing" their Rhythm Sticks. Play a variety of music – fast, slow, loud, quiet.

☺ Skills: Listed at front of Music Section.

✂ Materials To Be Used: Rhythm Sticks

✐ Teacher's Notes: Discussion on results of activity; open format; Teacher records own results.

Part 6
Creative Dramatics

Creative Dramatics

In Creative Dramatics
    We share our ideas
        And express
            Our emotions
                In this Art's
                    Panaceas;

For we use
    All our muscles,
        Our minds,
            And our talent,
                To dramatize life, ...,
                    ... It can truly
                        Be gallant!!

Vanessa Conaway Pace

Introduction To Creative Dramatics

Creative Dramatics is valuable in the preschool curriculum because it provides an opportunity for social, emotional, physical, and intellectual expression by the individual, as well as the group.

The children learn many social interaction skills. They cooperate with others, share a common physical space, share ideas, and take turns. Many opportunities are provided for emotional expression. As children practice positive social interaction and varied means of emotional expression they become better able to use these skills outside the classroom.

As Creative Dramatics encourages social and emotional growth, it also enhances the development of physical skills. The desire for expression through the body is strong in young children. Movement is a natural outlet for thinking and feeling.

To provide the best conditions for large free movements, the Teacher/caregiver's first concern is with large muscle development. In addition, an understanding of time, space, rhythm, and body relationship is essential for the direction of physical expression. When children are able to do activities involving these areas they gain mastery over their bodies.

Finally, Creative Dramatics stimulates intellectual development. The activities focus thought and discipline the mind. The demand for imagining environment, characters, and events sharpens memory skills and evokes originality, fluency, flexibility, and elaboration.

Within the framework of Creative Dramatics a child can explore and express feelings and emotions in a familiar and accepting environment. This will provide the background for healthy emotional expression in later life.

Creative Dramatics

Part 1   Free and Imitative Play in Speech and Movement

Skills To Develop

Child's Personality
- Physically
- Socially
- Intellectually

- Emotionally

Opportunities for growth in group participation

Activities – Overview

Movement Games – Dances
Home Center, Sharing Activities
Language – Act out stories; Make up stories; Problem solving; Listen to stories
Express inner feelings through finger plays, dance, puppets, free play
Games, Dances, Songs, and Activities done together

Equipment:

   Puppets, Finger Plays, Story Books, Games, Dance.

Objectives:
- To develop physical control;
- To maintain a strong healthy mind and body;
- To learn new body movements;
- To develop imagination;
- To express ideas through free play and movement;
- To learn how to cooperate with others;
- To learn how to share ideas, space, and materials with those around us.

Ideas for Room Arrangement: Creative Dramatics

Most Creative Dramatics will be done as a group activity during Gathering Time. A mid-morning time works well for these activities.

Puppets should be made by the teacher. Scrap material - 2 pieces - large enough to fit a childs hand are cut into puppet shape. Then sew up sides. Draw on face.

More Activities:

- Puppets – Stage or Circle Play
- Dance – Group – Free and Round Dances
- Plays – Programs
- Stories for dramatization
- Finger Plays

Creative Dramatics

I. Songs

A. I'm A Little Teapot

Words	Actions
I'm a little teapot,	
Short and stout,	
Here is my handle,	Put one hand on hip.
Here is my spout.	Hold out the other arm as a spout.
When I get all steamed up	
Then I shout, "Just	
Tip me over and pour me out."	Tip slowly to the side of the outstretched arm.

I'm a Little Teapot

Creative Dramatics

I. Songs (Continued)

B. <u>If You're Happy and You Know It</u>

Words	Actions
If you're happy and you know it, Clap your hands	Clap, clap
If you're happy and you know it, Clap your hands	Clap, clap
If you're happy and you know it, Then you're face will surely show it If you're happy and you know it, Clap your hands.	Clap, clap.

Other verses: 1. Touch your nose; 2. Show a smile; 3. Tap your knees
4. Stamp your feet; 5. Sing real loud; 6. Sing real soft
7. Turn around.

If You're Happy and You Know It

☺ <u>Skills:</u> Listed at front of Creative Dramatics Section.

✂ <u>Materials To Be Used:</u> Your Body; Your Voice; Your Imagination.

✎ <u>Teacher's Notes:</u> Discussion on results of activity; open format; Teacher records own results.

Creative Dramatics

2. Poetry

A. <u>Raining (Rhoda W. Bacmeister)</u>

    It's raining, raining, raining,
    And all the world is wet.
    It rained last night, and now today,
    It's raining, raining, yet!

B. <u>Whirl and Twirl</u>

    Like a leaf or a feather,
    In the windy, windy weather;
    We will whirl around,
    And twirl around
    And all sink down together.

C. <u>Brooms (Dorothy Aldis)</u>

    On stormy days
    When the wind is high
    Tall trees are brooms
    Sweeping the sky.

    They swish their branches
    In buckets of rain,
    And swash and sweek it
    Blue again.

Creative Dramatics

2. Poetry (Continued)

D. <u>My Shadow (Robert Louis Stevenson)</u>

I have a little shadow that goes in and out with me,
And what can be the use of him is more than I can see.
He is very, very like me from the heels up to the head;
And I see him jump before me, when I jump into my bed.

The funniest thing about him is the way he likes to grow—
Not at all like proper children, which is always very slow;
Fore he sometimes shoots up taller, like an India rubber ball,
And he sometimes gets so little, that there's none of him at all.

He hasn't got a notion of how children ought to play,
And can only make a fool of me in every sort of way.
He stays so close beside me, he's a coward you can see;
I'd think shame to stick to nursies, as that shadow sticks to me!

One morning, very early before the sun was up,
I rose and found the shining dew on every buttercup;
But my lazy little shadow, like an errant sleepyhead,
Had stayed at home behind me, and was fast asleep in bed.

☺ <u>Skills:</u> Listed at front of Creative Dramatics Section.

✄ <u>Materials To Be Used:</u> Your Body; your imagination.

✎ <u>Teacher's Notes:</u> Discussion on results of activity; open format; Teacher records own results.

Creative Dramatics

3. Finger Plays

A. <u>Can You Make a Rabbit?</u>

Can you make a rabbit with two ears, so very long?
And let him hop, hop, hop about on legs so small and strong.
He nibbles, bibbles carrots for his dinner every day.
As soon as he has had enough, he scampers far away.

    (Inserting the second finger of the left hand for the carrot between the thumb and fourth and fifth fingers of the right hand (mouth) open and close to imitate nibbling.)

B. <u>Ten Little Fingers</u>

I have 10 little fingers
And they all belong to me.
I can make them do things
Would you like to see?
I can shut them up tight
I can open them wide.
I can put them together
I can make them all hide.
I can make them jump high
I can make them jump low.
I can fold them up quietly
And hold them just so.

☺ <u>Skills:</u> Listed at front of Creative Dramatics Section.

✂ <u>Materials To Be Used:</u> Your Body; your imagination.

✎ <u>Teacher's Notes:</u> Discussion on results of activity; open format; Teacher records own results.

Creative Dramatics

3. Finger Plays (Continued)

C. <u>Where Is Thumbkin?</u>

Words	Actions
Where is Thumbkin?	
Where is Thumbkin?	
Here I am	Hold up one thumb.
Here I am.	Hold up other thumb.
How are you today, Sir?	Wiggle one thumb at the other.
Very fine, I thank you.	
Run away. Run away.	Hide behind back.

Do the same movements with Pointer, Tall Man, Ring Man, and Pinky.

Where Is Thumbkin?

Creative Dramatics

3. Finger Plays (Continued)

<u>D. Two Little Blackbirds</u>

Words	Actions
Two little blackbirds sitting on a hill	Place forefinger of each hand on shoulder.
One named Jack	Hold one finger out.
The other named Jill.	Hold out other finger.
Fly away, Jack. Fly away, Jill!	Make one hand and then the other "fly away".
Come back, Jack. Come back, Jill!	Bring hands back to shoulders one at a time.

☺ <u>Skills:</u> Listed at front of Creative Dramatics Section.

✂ <u>Materials To Be Used:</u> Your Body; your imagination.

✎ <u>Teacher's Notes:</u> Discussion on results of activity; open format; Teacher records own results.

Creative Dramatics

4. Paper Puppets

Directions: Cut out picture of a person, animals, or anything of interest, found in magazines, catalogues, etc. Let the child glue his picture on the cardboard backing, then glue stick to backside of cardboard.

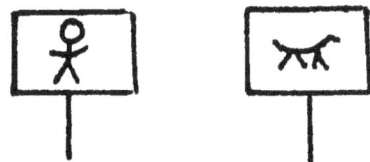

☺ <u>Skills:</u> Used for developing child's imagination, as well as free play and movement.

✄ <u>Materials To Be Used:</u> Old magazines or catalogues; Cardboard; Sticks (size large enough for child to hold and to glue picture from magazine on one end)

✎ <u>Teacher's Notes:</u> Discussion on results of activity; open format; Teacher records own results.

Creative Dramatics

5. Puppet Exercises

1. Practice everything that each of the following animals can do: Mouse, Rooster, Horse, Lion, Elephant; add some others.
2. Practice all the ways that people use their voices.
3. Practice all the ways that people can move.
4. Try these puppet actions (without props, except for puppet):

- Lift something heavy -light;
- Bounce a ball;
- Drive a car - fast/slow;
- Sit down - lie down;
- Fall down - roll over;
- Go to sleep;
- Wake up;
- Set the table;
- Pour water - drink it;
- Do exercises;
- Act frightened;
- Bow - nod;
- Cry - cover eyes;
- Act angry;
- Act sad;
- Scratch ear - nose;
- Pick flower;
- Stir cake;
- Search for something;
- Throw a kiss

Work with a puppet and puppet friend, and do the following (Or, you be the puppet's friend):

- Talk together;
- Dance together;
- Comb another's hair;
- Comfort crying puppet;
- Shake hands;
- Carry something together;
- Hand objects back and forth;
- Whisper together;
- Add more ideas of your own.

☺ <u>Skills:</u> Used for developing child's imagination, as well as free play and movement.

✂ <u>Materials To Be Used:</u> Depends upon the type of puppet you make.

✐ <u>Teacher's Notes:</u> Discussion on results of activity; open format; Teacher records own results

Creative Dramatics

6. Other Puppet Ideas

1. <u>Sock Puppet:</u>   Sock with eyes painted or sewn on.

2. <u>Mouth Puppet:</u>   Make of durable and washable materials.

3. <u>Plate Puppet:</u>   Face drawn on paper plate.

4. <u>Stick Puppet:</u>   Tongue depressor or stick with a Puppet-shape attached to one end.

5. <u>Hand or Finger Puppets:</u>   Made with fabric or paper.

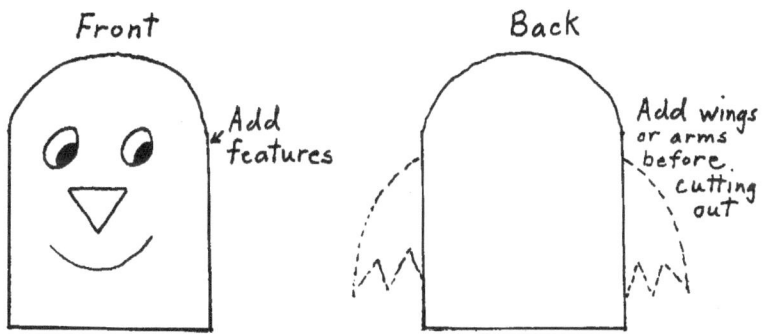

Hand or Finger Puppets
Secure Fabric halves with "Tacky" or fabric Glue
A heavy fabric like felt should be used.

✐ <u>Teacher's Notes:</u>   Discussion on results of activity; open format; Teacher records own results.

Creative Dramatics

7. Dancing

<u>Choreographed and Spontaneous Dancing:</u> Singing simple folksongs, children make up dances using scarves or paper streamers for added fun.

- ☺ <u>Skills:</u> Used for developing child's imagination, coordination, self image, and self confidence, awareness of self in space, relationship of self to things, as well as free play and movement. Choreographed dancing teaches patterning, sequencing, memory, cooperation, following directions, sense of community, history.

- ✂ <u>Materials To Be Used:</u> Scarves and streamers

- ✎ <u>Teacher's Notes:</u> Discussion on results of activity; open format; Teacher records own results.

Creative Dramatics

8. Games

<u>A. Imitating Animals:</u> One child imitates an animal, and the others must guess the animal.

☺ <u>Skills:</u> As listed on the first page of Creative Dramatics Section.

✂ <u>Materials To Be Used:</u> Use your imagination!

✎ <u>Teacher's Notes:</u> Discussion on results of activity; open format; Teacher records own results.

Creative Dramatics

8. Games (Continued)

B. <u>Balance Beam</u>: Place the Balance Beam on the floor for balancing. Let the children pretend it is a high wire they are crossing, or a bridge over a stream, or, imagine they are a train on the tracks (train wheels *never* leave the tracks!). Or, what else can they be??

☺ <u>Skills:</u> As listed on the first page of Creative Dramatics Section.

✂ <u>Materials To Be Used:</u> Balance beam, 6 to 8 feet long, 4 inches wide; your imagination.

✎ <u>Teacher's Notes:</u> Discussion on results of activity; open format; Teacher records own results.

Creative Dramatics

8. Games (Continued)

C. <u>Beans (rocks, seeds, water)</u>: Place a small dish and some beans at one end of the room, and at the other end of the room an empty saucer. Let each child see how many beans he can scoop on a spoon in two turns and carry across to the empty saucer.

☺ <u>Skills:</u> As listed on the first page of the Creative Dramatics Section.

✂ <u>Materials To Be Used:</u> Beans (rocks, seeds, water), spoon, dish.

✐ <u>Teacher's Notes:</u> Discussion on results of activity; open format; Teacher records own results.

Creative Dramatics

8. Games (Continued)

D. Dress-up/Imagination Center: Children love to dress up and roll play. Provide a corner area of the room where you keep a box of a few old clothes, scarves, etc. Let 2 or 3 children at a time use the corner area to pretend and make-believe. A small table and a couple of chairs could be added also. Give children turns in the area.

☺ <u>Skills:</u> As listed on the first page of Creative Dramatics Section.

✂ <u>Materials To Be Used:</u> Box of old clothes, scarves, etc.; containers for food preparation; small table and two chairs; pretend food; lots of imagination.

✎ <u>Teacher's Notes:</u> Discussion on results of activity; open format; Teacher records own results.

Creative Dramatics

9. Stories and Plays

Select good stories to read to the children. Stories can develop imagination, wonder, and enjoyment in the life of a child. Children love stories. Don't hesitate to re-read their favorite stories to them.

Story-time can be a cozy, warm experience.

Simple stories allow children to act out/roll play the characters in the story.

Children enjoy participating in singing, acting out, and roll playing.

They also enjoy making up their *own* stories and telling them to others. Or, acting out their own stories with others' help.

☺ <u>Skills:</u> As listed on the first page of Creative Dramatics Section.

✂ <u>Materials To Be Used:</u> Stories, songs, and plays (oral and written).

✎ <u>Teacher's Notes:</u> Discussion on results of activity; open format; Teacher records own results.

www.fortheloveofchildrenbook.com   E-mail: info@.fortheloveofchildrenbook.com

Part 7
Language Arts

Language Arts

In Language Arts
    We learn how to speak; ...
        First there's one word,
            Then two, ...,
                ... It takes more
                    Than a squeak,

To communicate
    All these ideas
        That we're getting,
            As we explore life
                In our new
                    Earth-bound setting!

Vanessa Conaway Pace

Introduction To Language Arts

The spoken vocabulary of preschool-age children increases rapidly when exposed to ever-widening vocabulary. The average preschool-age child adds about fifty new words to his vocabulary each month. By age five he should be able to use about two thousand words. A child's understanding of vocabulary precedes and exceeds his use of words. That is, he understands what is said to him before he is able to use the words spoken to him.

While developing vocabulary the child learns to combine words to form sentences. Short sentences of three or four words, consisting primarily of nouns and verbs, appear first during the preschool years. Later a child adds more words, and his sentence structure becomes more sophisticated. Opportunities to talk, and to hear others converse, help children to develop language skill. Of course, the more varied a child's experiences are, the more he talks. Most children enjoy talking to each other. Social contacts in which conversation takes place help a child to know himself and others better.

Hearing good speech is more helpful to a child than learning grammar rules. Preschoolers learn to pronounce and use words by imitating the speech around them. Caregivers and parents should make a conscious effort to speak properly in the presence of children. They should avoid talking down to children.

Language Arts activities enable children to develop listening and speaking skills in a fun, age-appropriate way. Many of the Language Arts skills are integrated into other sections of this book. The development of language is vital in all areas of a child's life. Skills in speech awareness, imitation, judgement and self-confidence are just a few of these areas.

Language Arts

Listening   Reading   Writing

<u>Skills To Develop</u>

- Build Vocabulary

- Looking at books
- Develop large motor

- Develop fine muscle control
- Eye Development through hand activities
- Hearing sounds correctly

- Recognize own name

<u>Activities – Overview</u>

Listening to stories, and poetry; Singing songs
Library Corner
Physical Outside Activities (See Physical Activities Section.)
Drawing and Sorting Games
Sandpaper Letter Flash Cards: Child traces letter with finger.
Repeating phonetic sounds of letters; Flash cards; Alphabet chart; Gathering Game
Post name on child's desk and things

<u>Equipment:</u>

Hands on: Sorting, Sand tray, Magazines and books of all kinds to look at.

<u>Objectives:</u>

- Prepare an environment that encourages communication skills;
- Eye-hand coordination – Perception and Sequencing;
- Learning concepts: Top, Bottom, Front, Back, Left, Right;
- Recognizing letters and related sounds;
- Build Listening skills through listening to teacher's directions, stories read; Speaking in terms of personal needs or interest;
- Expressing own thoughts, feelings, ideas, and respecting those of others.

Ideas for Room Arrangement: Language Arts

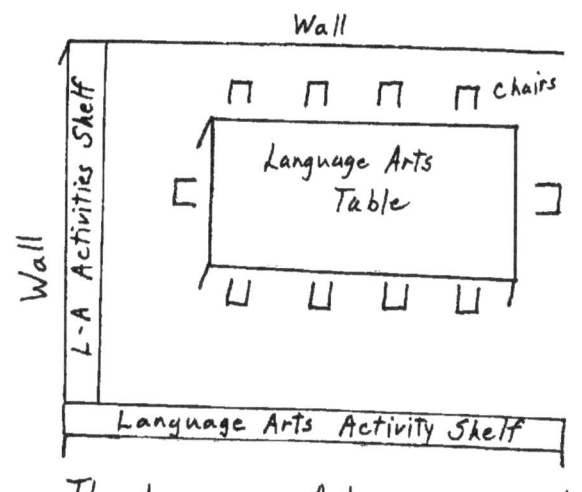

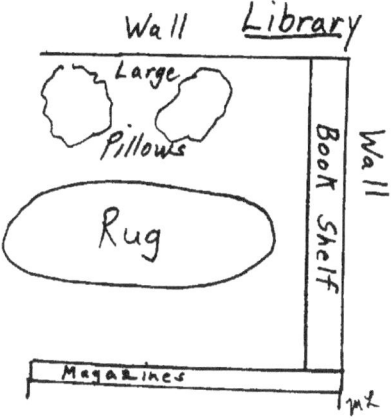

The Language Arts area may be set up anywhere in the room.

The Library area should be set up in a quiet area if at all possible.

More Activities:

- Small sand container to make letters in the sand gently shaking container
- Alphabet Flash Cards;
- Alphabet Songs to sing;
- Flash Card Game – Lay out cards in alphabetical order;
- Write letters over dotted lines with crayon or pencil;

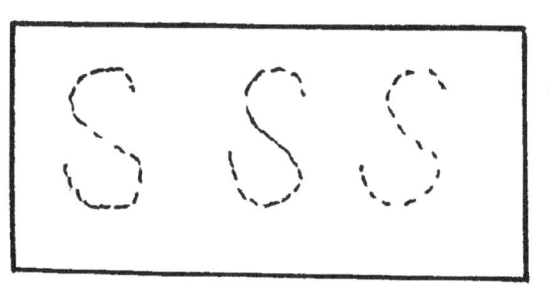

Dotted Letters

Language Arts Projects

1. <u>Making A "Picture File"</u>:

    From various magazines make a variety of "Picture Files" to be used during Gathering Time. Bring a particular Picture File to the Circle. Show the pictures one by one. Let the children share what they see. The Teacher can fill in additional insights.

    Suggestions for Picture Files: Animals, Weather, Seasons, Children.

    ☺ <u>Skills:</u> As listed at the front of the Language Arts Section.

    ✂ <u>Materials To Be Used:</u> Magazine Pictures

    ✎ <u>Teacher's Notes:</u> Discussion on results of activity; open format; Teacher records own results.

Language Arts Projects

2. <u>Color Chart Activity:</u>

    ⇨ Display on the wall a Color Chart with basic colors: Red, Green, Blue, Yellow, White, Black, Brown;

    ⇨ Cut out 2 inch by 2 inch squares of construction paper of basic colors – enough to give one square to each child. During Gathering Time have each child in turn come up to chart and match the color. Help the child identify the matching color by its name. (Teacher may help by naming the color.)

☺ <u>Skills:</u> As listed at the front of the Language Arts Section.

✂ <u>Materials To Be Used:</u> Color Chart; Small colored paper squares.

✐ <u>Teacher's Notes:</u> Discussion on results of activity; open format; Teacher records own results.

Language Arts Projects

3. <u>Stop and Tell:</u>

    ⇨ Teacher explains to children that together they are going to make up a story;

    ⇨ The Teacher begins the story by writing 2 or 3 sentences on the chalkboard or on a large piece of paper;

    ⇨ The Teacher then invites the children to give their ideas to continue the middle and ending of the story;

    ⇨ The Story can be put up on the wall and re-read to the children who made up their very own story.

☺ <u>Skills:</u> As listed at the front of the Language Arts Section.

✂ <u>Materials To Be Used:</u> Blackboard and Chalk; or, Paper and Black Crayon.

✎ <u>Teacher's Notes:</u> Discussion on results of activity; open format; Teacher records own results.

Language Arts Projects

4. <u>Listening To Stories: (Gathering Time/Circle Time):</u>

   During the school day the children should be read to at least once or twice. Good stories are vital to language development.

☺ <u>Skills:</u> As listed at the front of the Language Arts Section.

✂ <u>Materials To Be Used:</u> Reading List of Children's Books.

✎ <u>Teacher's Notes:</u> Discussion on results of activity; open format; Teacher records own results.

Language Arts Projects

5. <u>Discussion About Friends:</u>

During Gathering Time ask the children if they know about being a friend:

- ➪ What is a friend?
- ➪ How do you become a friend to someone? (sharing, helping, saying kind words, doing kind deeds, ...)
- ➪ How can we be friends with each other in the classroom; at home; ...?
- ➪ Read a story about Friends: Some suggested books:
    - ➪ "A Friend Is Someone Who Likes You" - Anglund
    - ➪ "Do You Want To Be My Friend?" - Carle
    - ➪ "Play With Me" - Ets
    - ➪ "George and Martha" - Marshall

☺ <u>Skills:</u> As listed at the front of the Language Arts Section.

✂ <u>Materials To Be Used:</u> Books on Friends, about people or animals.

✎ <u>Teacher's Notes:</u> Discussion on results of activity; open format; Teacher records own results.

Language Arts Projects

6. <u>Animals and Their Babies:</u>

During Gathering Time show pictures of animals to the children. Discuss how in the Spring many animals have their babies. Show pictures of babies. Talk about the animals – where they live, what they eat, ... Showing and discussing pictures builds the children's vocabulary.

Then play the following game:

>Little Woolly Lamb likes to sleep, play and walk.
>Pet it gently: It will talk: "Baa, Baa, Baa".

>Second Verse: Little Downy Duckling ... "Quack, Quack, Quack".
>Third Verse: Little Fluffy Chick ... "Peep, Peep, Peep".
>Fourth Verse: Little Furry Kitten ... "Meow, Meow, Meow".

Teacher recites first three lines of the verse, and the children add the sound that baby animal makes. Continue with animals the children name.

<u>Variation:</u> Children can take turns being the animal once the animal's characteristics have been discussed.

☺ <u>Skills:</u> As listed at the front of the Language Arts Section.

✄ <u>Materials To Be Used:</u> Pictures of animals; Stories about animals.

✎ <u>Teacher's Notes:</u> Discussion on results of activity; open format; Teacher records own results.

Language Arts Projects

7. <u>Group Language Games</u>:

   A. <u>Charades:</u>

   ⇨ One child acts out an activity;
   ⇨ The other children guess what he is doing.

   B. <u>Telephone Game</u>:

   ⇨ Children sit in a circle;
   ⇨ The Teacher/Caregiver whispers something in the first child's ear;
   ⇨ That child whispers it in the ear of the child next to him, etc.;
   ⇨ The last child in the circle says it out loud;
   ⇨ The goal is for what he says to be the same thing that the Teacher/Caregiver said.

   C. <u>What Are You Wearing?"</u>

   ⇨ The children sit in a circle;
   ⇨ The Teacher/Caregiver asks the question, "What are you wearing? If you are wearing shoes, etc., please stand up."
   ⇨ After those children stand up, the Teacher/Caregiver tells them to sit down;
   ⇨ Then the game is repeated.

   D. <u>I Spy:</u>
   ⇨ Teacher/Caregiver says, "I spy, with my little eye _____ (names some object everyone can see)."
   ⇨ Then the children try to guess what object she sees.

Language Arts Projects

7. Group Language Games (Continued):

  E. <u>Marching Around the Alphabet/Numbers/Shapes/Colors:</u>

  ⇨ Teacher puts on the floor six-to-ten cards (one card per child) with different letters of the alphabet, numbers, shapes, or colors printed on them (one per card);

  ⇨ Teacher tells the children, "March, march, march, ..., stop.";

  ⇨ Child picks up the card he/she has stopped by;

  ⇨ Then the Teacher calls each child in turn to name the letter and/or the sound, number, shape, or color on the card;

  ⇨ Then the child places the card on the floor and sits in the Circle, and the Teacher selects another six-to-ten children to do the same game;

  ⇨ The cards may be varied by the Teacher in each game.

☺ <u>Skills:</u> As listed at the front of the Language Arts Section.

✂ <u>Materials To Be Used:</u> Cards with alphabet, numbers, shapes, or colors on them.

✐ <u>Teacher's Notes:</u> Discussion on results of activity; open format; Teacher records own results.

Language Arts Projects

8. <u>Land or Sea</u>:

　　⇨　Discuss Land and Sea (show pictures).
　　⇨　Take a walk and collect small samples of dirt/land growth (rocks, grass, etc.).
　　⇨　Visit a body of water and collect a jar of water.
　　⇨　During Gathering Time/Circle Time talk about land and water:

　　　　⇨ How they are used by us;
　　　　⇨ What lives on land and in the water;
　　　　⇨ What items relate to land and to water?

　　⇨　Play a Land and Water (Sea) Game: Name items related to land and sea:

　　　　⇨　If the item relates to water (sea) the player pretends to swim;
　　　　⇨　If the item relates to land the player pretends to hike.

☺ <u>Skills</u>: As listed at the front of the Language Arts Section.

✂ <u>Materials To Be Used</u>: Collection of land and water samples; Pictures of land and water (sea); Books; Magazines.

✎ <u>Teacher's Notes</u>: Discussion on results of activity; open format; Teacher records own results.

Language Arts Projects

9. Learning Alphabet Letters:

Post Alphabet on the wall. Make matching letter flash cards. During Gathering/Circle Time play the Alphabet Game. Introduce new letter of the week (letter and its sound). Let the children find the letter on the wall chart. Then let each child come up to the alphabet line. Hand him or her a flash card. Let the child find the letter on the wall chart and say the corresponding sound. (Use only the letters already presented to the group.) Help the child to find the letter and say the sound (if necessary).

NOTE: The Alphabet Flash Cards can be made available to the children by placing them in the "Language Area" on a shelf. During class time, when the children can select what activity they want to play with, they may use the available Flash Cards - matching them to the Wall Chart. (This game can be played alone or with a friend.)

☺ Skills: As listed at the front of the Language Arts Section.

✂ Materials To Be Used: Alphabet Wall Chart; Alphabet Flash Cards.

✎ Teacher's Notes: Discussion on results of activity; open format; Teacher records own results.

Language Arts Projects

10. <u>Learning Numbers: 1-10</u>:

Post Numbers Chart on the wall. Make matching number flash cards. During Gathering/Circle Time play the Number Game. Introduce new number of the week. Let the children find the number on the wall chart. Then let each child come up to the number line. Hand him or her a flash card. Let the child find the number on the wall chart and say the name of the number. (Use only the numbers already presented to the group.) Help the child to find the number and say the name (if necessary).

<u>NOTE</u>: The Number Flash Cards can be made available to the children by placing them in the "Language Area" on a shelf. During class time, when the children can select what activity they want to play with, they may use the available Flash Cards – matching them to the Wall Chart. (This game can be played alone or with a friend.)

☺ <u>Skills:</u> As listed at the front of the Language Arts Section.

✂ <u>Materials To Be Used:</u> Number Chart and Flash Cards.

✏ <u>Teacher's Notes:</u> Discussion on results of activity; open format; Teacher records own results.

Language Arts Projects

11. <u>Shape Boxes:</u>

    The child sorts the shape cards into the boxes with matching shapes.

    A first game might be made with a color on each box, and matching shapes on a set of cards to be sorted by the child into the boxes.

    <u>Letter Boxes:</u>

    Set up the same as above. The Letter Boxes are to be used after children are familiar with Shape Boxes.

    ☺ <u>Skills:</u> Recognizing similarities and differences; Observing shape and letter forms; Matching; Making comparisons.

    ✄ <u>Materials To Be Used:</u> Empty ½ pint milk cartons, tops removed; Paper to cover cartons; Marking Pen or Crayon to make shapes or write letters; Tagboard strips 1 ½ inches X 6 inches (five to ten for each Shape or Letter in the series; Container for cards; Container for Shape or Letter Boxes and Boxed Cards.

    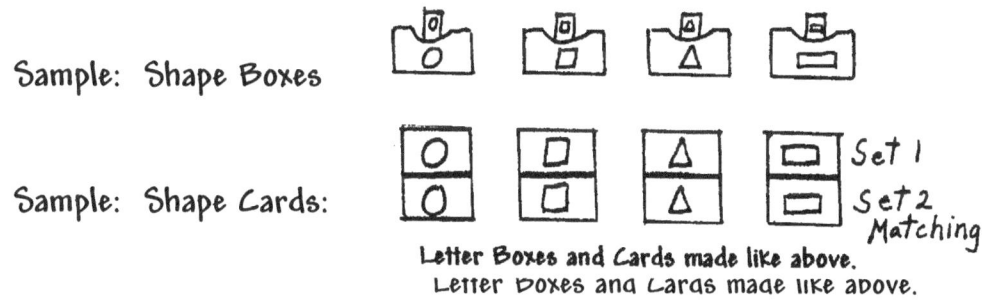

    Sample: Shape Boxes

    Sample: Shape Cards:

    Letter Boxes and Cards made like above.

    ✏ <u>Teacher's Notes:</u> Discussion on results of activity; open format; Teacher records own results.

Language Arts Projects

12. Sandpaper Letters:

This exercise is an extension of the games of Letter Matching, (matching Letters written on cards with those on Letter Boxes, and, also, those written on Flash Cards with the Alphabet Wall Chart). These individual Letter Cards - lower case and capital letters - are made out of sandpaper that has been glued on Tagboard or heavy weight paper.

The Teacher presents one letter at a time to the child - showing the child how to trace over the sandpaper-letter shape with 2 fingers (pointer and index fingers). While tracing over the letter shape the child repeats the phonetic sound. Lower case letters are presented first.

☺ Skills: Remote preparation for writing letters; Remote preparation for reading; Hand-eye coordination development; Relating sound of letter to shape of letter.

✂ Materials To Be Used: Sandpaper; Tagboard or Heavy Paper for making cards; Glue.

Sample Letter: [A] Card

✎ Teacher's Notes: Discussion on results of activity; open format; Teacher records own results.

Language Arts

Sample Phonetic Sounds

Used for presentation in Matching Letter Games and Sandpaper Letter Game.

A	As in cat	N	As in nap
B	As in bat	O	As in ox
C	As in cow	P	As in pat
D	As in dog	Q	As in quit
E	As in bed	R	As in red
F	As in fox	S	As in sad
G	As in got	T	As in top
H	As in hop	U	As in up
I	As in it	V	As in van
J	As in jump	W	As in wet
K	As in kit	X	As in box
L	As in lip	Y	As in yet
M	As in map	Z	As in zap

Language Arts

Sample Printed Letters

Used for Matching Letter Games and Sandpaper Letter Game

A	a
B	b
C	c
D	d
E	e
F	f
G	g
H	h
I	i
J	j
K	k
L	l
M	m
N	n
O	o
P	p
Q	q
R	r
S	s
T	t
U	u
V	v
W	w
X	x
Y	y
Z	**z**

Part 8
Arts and Crafts

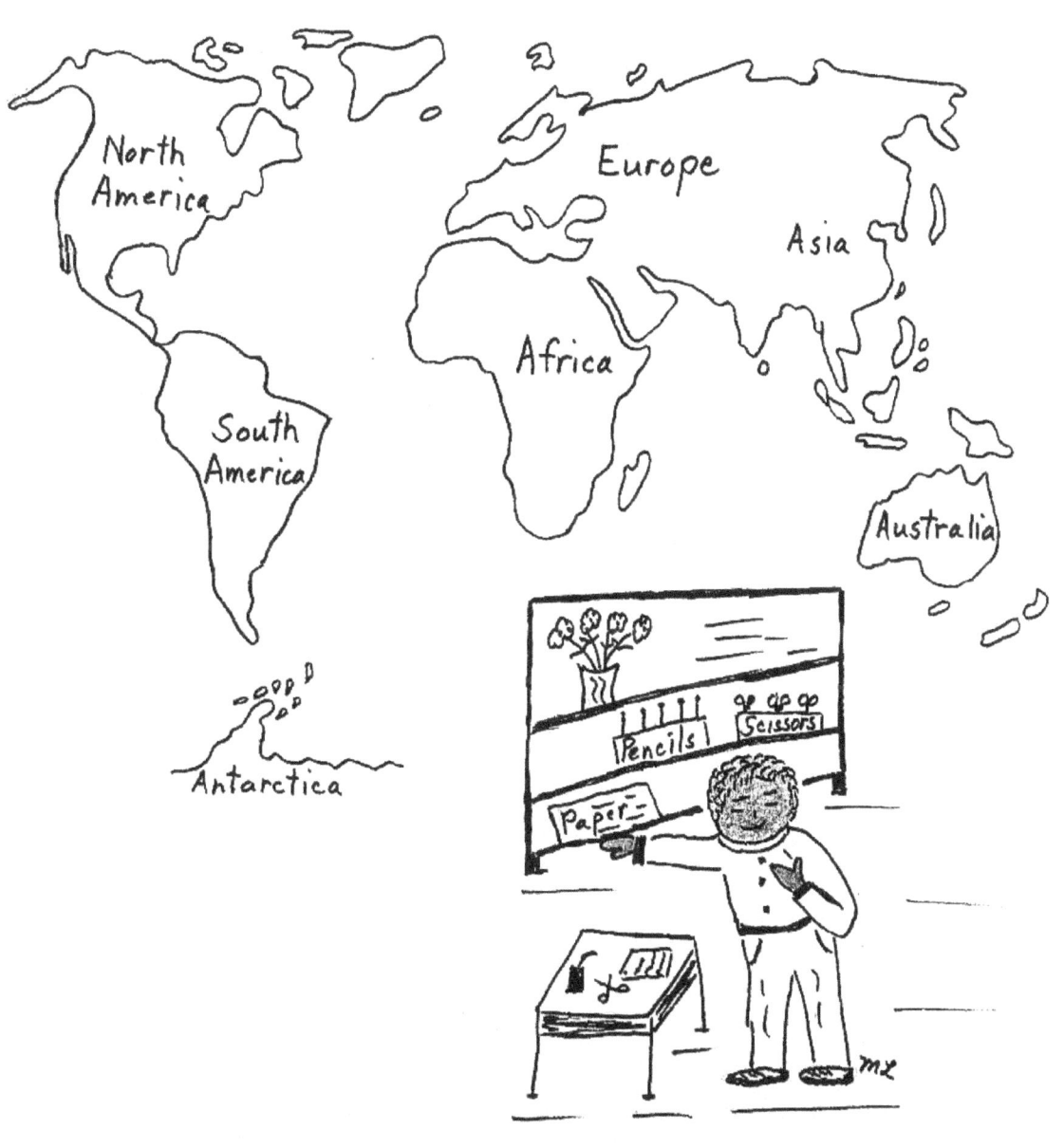

Arts and Crafts

In Arts and Crafts
    We are truly
        "Unique";
            For its more
                About "us"
                    Than about
                        Our "technique";

For its here
    That we learn
        To express
            Who we are,
                While developing skills
                    That will take "us"
                      Quite far!

Vanessa Conaway Pace

Introduction To Arts and Crafts

Arts and crafts activities for a preschool child serve to introduce the child to a variety of art media. Sometimes the child uses his or her hands directly with such materials as clay, dough, paste, finger paints, and materials of different textures. At other times they use brushes, scissors, and carpentry tools, and gradually they develop some skill in manipulation. But, the main function of art is to serve as an avenue through which the children can express themselves and release their feelings. Anxious attention to the product, rather than the process, should be discouraged. Art is an important means of expression.

A few things to remember:

1. Each child comes to us with his own tastes;
2. We should encourage inventiveness and individual outlook;
3. Do not expect preschool children to concentrate over long periods;
4. Do not expect preschool children to create detailed designs;
5. Do not be overly concerned about technique;
6. Scribbling is an important activity; children *need* to do it. It is one of the first means of non-verbal expression. The thorough exploration of scribbling is a prerequisite for all subsequent activity in art;
7. If a child leaves off the ears or nose on the head, or if he makes the parts in incorrect proportions – this is as it should be! You should not attempt to "fix" this drawing and tell him how things should be. It is imperative at this stage of development that the child feel free to create symbols as they occur to him, without any awareness of possible adult standards of "right and wrong". Failure to acknowledge this can inhibit and dissuade a child from further personal expression.
8. *Art activities should be fun!*

As we work with children, the use of art media should be viewed as a means of self-expression. If this avenue is safeguarded children will use art as an outlet for creativity and feelings, and the *process* will be the important factor, not the *product*.

Arts and Crafts

Crayons   Pencils   Scissors   Paste   Clay   Sand

<u>Skills To Develop</u>
- Hand-Eye Coordination
- Developing Small Muscles

- Experiencing Different Textures

- Developing Concepts of Shape, Size, and Colors
- Expressing Feelings, Creativity and Imagination

<u>*Activities – Overview*</u>
- Scissors cutting; Coloring a picture
  - Scissors work; Clay work; Ruler work; Using Crayons and Pencils
- Collage work involving use of nature (leaves, sand, rocks, ...,) and man-made fabrics (paper, materials, ...,)
- Coloring, Drawing, Observing Shapes in Nature
- Clay work; Coloring; ...;

<u>Equipment:</u>

    Pencils, Crayons, Rulers, Scissors, Paper, Magazines, Paste Recipe, Trays for Sand Drawing.

<u>Objectives:</u>

- Building of self confidence through simple tasks;
- Strengthening of hand-eye coordination;
- Strengthening small hand muscles;
- Appreciation of arts and crafts made by myself and with others.

Arts and Crafts

Ideas for Room Arrangement: Arts and Crafts Centers

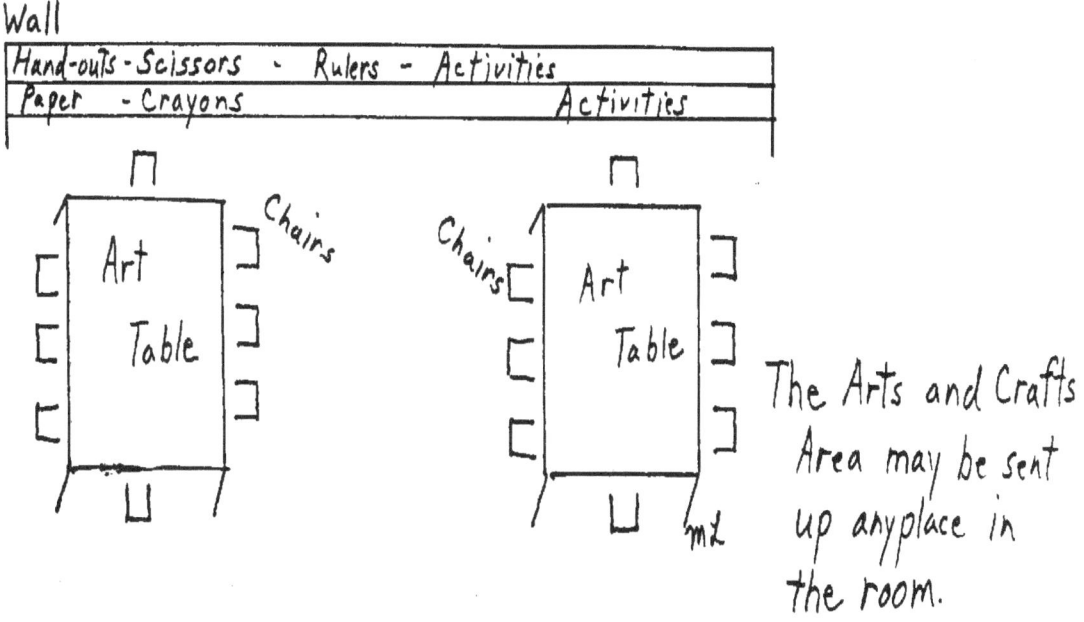

More Activities:

- Cutting on line, straight, curved, etc.;
- Collaging;
- Shapes – Cut out and glue;
- Local clay and paste recipe;
- Painting – water colors, tempura;
- Crayons, colored pencils, chalk;
- Coloring, drawing, sketching.

Arts and Crafts Projects

1. <u>Paper Collage:</u>

Show the children how to tear paper, using thumb and index finger grasp with both hands, side-by-side, and pulling in opposite directions. Let the children tear small pieces of paper (pictures from magazines or scrap colored paper). Then give each child a regular piece of paper. Place containers of paste within the children's reach. Let the children paste the torn papers on their large paper, making free, colorful collages.

☺ <u>Skills:</u> Listed at front of Arts and Crafts Section.

✂ <u>Materials To Be Used:</u> Paper and Paste.

✎ <u>Teacher's Notes:</u> Discussion on results of activity; open format; Teacher records own results.

Arts and Crafts Projects

2. <u>Nature Collage</u>

   Children take a nature walk and collect small leaves, grasses, flowers, etc., in a small paper bag. Upon returning to the classroom, gather the children in a circle and let the children show one or two things from their bags. Then let the children go to a table, and on a piece of heavy paper (construction paper quality) paste their nature treasures from their bags.

   ☺ <u>Skills:</u> Listed at front of Arts and Crafts Section.

   ✄ <u>Materials To Be Used:</u> Nature findings; Paper; Paste.

   ✎ <u>Teacher's Notes:</u> Discussion on results of activity; open format; Teacher records own results.

Arts and Crafts Projects

3. <u>Seed and Bean Collage:</u>

Bring a collection of various beans to the classroom. Let the children paste them on a heavy type of paper. Show the children various ideas in designs – lines, circles, zig-zags. They may or may not use these ideas.

☺ <u>Skills:</u> Listed at front of Arts and Crafts Section.

✄ <u>Materials To Be Used:</u> Seeds; Beans; Paste; Paper.

✎ <u>Teacher's Notes:</u> Discussion on results of activity; open format; Teacher records own results.

Arts and Crafts Projects

4. <u>Handprint Bird:</u>

   Lay the child's hand on the paper. Spread fingers, or keep fingers closed. Trace around the hand. Add eye and beak to the outline of the thumb. Brightly color the rest of the outlined fingers. Add legs below the outline of the palm. Children may draw one or more birds, using various colors.

   Sample: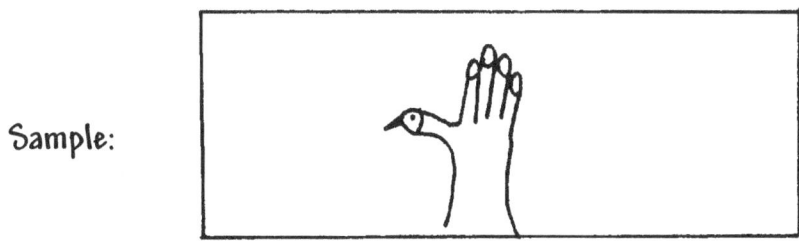

   ☺ <u>Skills:</u> Listed at front of Arts and Crafts Section.

   ✂ <u>Materials To Be Used:</u> Paper; Pencil; Crayons.

   ✐ <u>Teacher's Notes:</u> Discussion on results of activity; open format; Teacher records own results.

Arts and Crafts Projects

5. <u>Paper Bag Bird:</u>

   Stuff a lunch bag (small) half full of newspaper. Tie a string in the middle of the sack. Cut ½ inch wide strips for tail feathers. Cut to, but not through, string. Make cardboard head and tape to bag.

   Sample:

   ☺ <u>Skills:</u> Listed at front of Arts and Crafts Section.

   ✂ <u>Materials To Be Used:</u> Paper bag; String; Newspaper; Cardboard; Tape.

   ✎ <u>Teacher's Notes:</u> Discussion on results of activity; open format; Teacher records own results.

Arts and Crafts Projects

6. <u>Block Print with Potato:</u>

   Adult prepares potatoes. Cut potato in half. Remove background by cutting to design shape from outer edge of the potato. Prepare several potatoes with different designs (circle, square, triangle, and rectangle). Holding to half of potato, child dips design into paint tray and presses it onto a piece of paper.

   ☺ <u>Skills:</u> Listed at front of Arts and Crafts Section.

   ✄ <u>Materials To Be Used:</u> Knife (for Teacher's use only); Potatoes; Paint; Shallow Trays; Paper.

   ✐ <u>Teacher's Notes:</u> Discussion on results of activity; open format; Teacher records own results.

Arts and Crafts Projects

7. <u>Macaroni Necklaces:</u>

Cut piece of string 25 inches in length. Tie 1-inch piece of wood, or a large knot, at one end of the string to keep the macaroni from falling off. Wrap the other end of the string with tape to make a needle. String macaroni of various shapes to make a necklace. Remove the piece of wood and tie the ends of the string together when completed.

<u>Option:</u> If food coloring is available, dye the macaroni various colors before stringing. Let the children choose their colors and shapes before stringing.

☺ <u>Skills:</u> Listed at front of Arts and Crafts Section.

✂ <u>Materials To Be Used:</u> Macaroni; String; Small pieces of wood; Tape; Food Coloring (optional).

✎ <u>Teacher's Notes:</u> Discussion on results of activity; open format; Teacher records own results.

Arts and Crafts Projects

8. <u>Spring Baskets:</u>

Cover the bottom half of a milk carton, or any small carton, with decorated paper that has been colored by the child. Let the child fill the carton with dry grasses and colorful flowers to take home. A wonderful experience in showing love and learning to give!

☺ <u>Skills:</u> Listed at front of Arts and Crafts Section.

✂ <u>Materials To Be Used:</u> Milk Cartons; Paste; Paper.

✐ <u>Teacher's Notes:</u> Discussion on results of activity; open format; Teacher records own results.

Arts and Crafts Projects

9. <u>Headbands:</u>

Cut paper headband (about 1-½ inches wide). Adjust paper band to fit head, and staple. If staples are not available, make holes in the ends of the paper and attach the ends with string. Cut out two "rabbit" ears for each child. The child colors and pastes the ear on the headband. If the child is old enough, and is able, he or she may cut out their own rabbit ears after they are colored; otherwise, the Teacher needs to do the cutting. When headbands are completed various activities can be done during Gathering Time: Dancing, hopping to music, listening to the story of "Peter Rabbit", are a few suggestions.

☺ <u>Skills:</u> Listed at front of Arts and Crafts Section.

✂ <u>Materials To Be Used:</u> Paper Strips; Paper Ear Shapes; Scissors.

✎ <u>Teacher's Notes:</u> Discussion on results of activity; open format; Teacher records own results.

Arts and Crafts Projects

10. <u>Raindrop Design:</u>

    Use seeds as raindrops. Drop 5 to 10 seeds on the paper. Make dots where "raindrops" fall. Create design by connecting all the "raindrops".

    ☺ <u>Skills:</u> Listed at front of Arts and Crafts Section.

    ✂ <u>Materials To Be Used:</u> Seeds; Paper; Crayons

    ✎ <u>Teacher's Notes:</u> Discussion on results of activity; open format; Teacher records own results.

Arts and Crafts Projects

11. <u>Kite:</u>

Draw a diamond-shaped kite on a piece of paper. Cut or tear along the lines to make a kite. Attach a short piece of yarn to the kite. Tear pieces of paper and tape them to the yarn to make a tail. Attach a longer piece of yarn for the kite string. Children may decorate the kite by coloring it, painting it, collaging it, or anything else you can come up with.

☺ <u>Skills:</u> Listed at front of Arts and Crafts Section.

✂ <u>Materials To Be Used:</u> Paper; Scissors; Yarn or String; Tape; Crayons.

✎ <u>Teacher's Notes:</u> Discussion on results of activity; open format; Teacher records own results.

Arts and Crafts Projects

12. <u>Tree Drawing:</u>

Place forearm and hand with fingers spread on construction paper. Trace around the forearm and hand with brown crayon to make the tree trunk and branches. Color the tree and leaves with crayons.

Sample: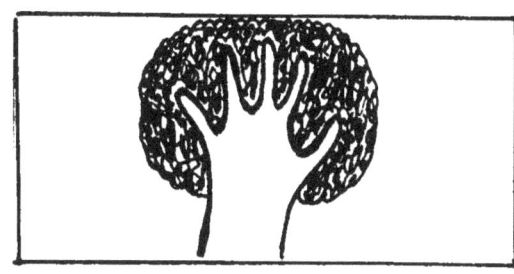

-  <u>Skills:</u> Listed at front of Arts and Crafts Section.

- ✂ <u>Materials To Be Used:</u> Paper; Crayons.

- ✎ <u>Teacher's Notes:</u> Discussion on results of activity; open format; Teacher records own results.

Arts and Crafts Projects

13. <u>Foot Butterfly</u>:

   Trace around shoes to make the wings. Draw the body between the wings. Add antennae. Color butterfly with crayons.

   Variation: Trace around feet instead of shoes.

   Samples: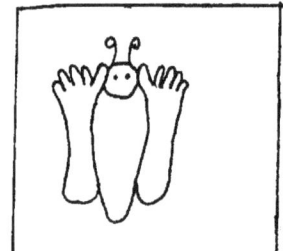

   ☺ <u>Skills:</u> Listed at front of Arts and Crafts Section.

   ✂ <u>Materials To Be Used:</u> Paper; Pencil; Crayons.

   ✏ <u>Teacher's Notes:</u> Discussion on results of activity; open format; Teacher records own results.

Arts and Crafts Projects

14. <u>Flying Bird:</u>

Cut bird and wings from construction paper. Color bird with crayons. Place wings through slot cut in bird's body.

Sample:

Wing

Paper folded in half.. Cut on the dotted line and then unfold.

☺ <u>Skills:</u> Listed at front of Arts and Crafts Section.

✄ <u>Materials To Be Used:</u> Construction Paper; Scissors; Crayons; String.

✎ <u>Teacher's Notes:</u> Discussion on results of activity; open format; Teacher records own results.

Arts and Crafts Projects

15. <u>Pebble Pictures:</u>

    Collect pebbles (very small rocks). Paste pebbles to a piece of cardboard to create a picture.

    Variation: Glue small pebbles together to form fish or animals. Allow glue to dry. Add facial features with crayons.

    ☺ <u>Skills:</u> Listed at front of Arts and Crafts Section.

    ✂ <u>Materials To Be Used:</u> Small Pebbles (Rocks); Cardboard; Crayons.

    ✎ <u>Teacher's Notes:</u> Discussion on results of activity; open format; Teacher records own results.

Arts and Crafts Projects

16. <u>Dough Letters:</u>

Pick a recipe from the Recipe Section (See Fundraiser Section Number 8) for Playdough, or Craft Dough. Allow children to form letters; cook it, or dry it, according to instructions; paint. Once completed, children can trace over letters with finger, or use letters to form simple words.

One fun activity is to have your class make an alphabet, and display it in the room, with each child's name above the letter they have created.

☺ <u>Skills:</u> Listed at front of Arts and Crafts Section.

✂ <u>Materials To Be Used:</u> See Individual Recipes; Paint.

✐ <u>Teacher's Notes:</u> Discussion on results of activity; open format; Teacher records own results.

www.fortheloveofchildrenbook.com   E-mail: info@.fortheloveofchildrenbook.com

Part 9
Physical Activities

Physical Activities

In Physical Activities
    We "play"
        Ourselves healthy; ...;
            Its "learning"
                That's cloaked
                    In some ways
                        That are stealthy!

We're developing skills
    Through our
        Physical Self
            That will help "us" create
                A "Whole" life
                    Full of wealth!!

Vanessa Conaway Pace

Introduction To Physical Activities

How can this strong foundation develop? What resources do young children have to build the basis for a happy, well-adjusted life? How can parents and teachers facilitate the child's successful achievement of developmental tasks? A noted authority on human development says:

Play is an essential to the development of a normal, well-adjusted personality. It provides the child with opportunities to develop physically, emotionally, socially and morally in a way that no other single type of activity can.

Play meets the needs of the young child. All aspects of development are stimulated by the child's play experiences.

Physical Development

Play supplies an outlet for young children to express their boundless physical energy. By continual repetition of a variety of movements in play, the child's muscles develop, and control and coordination of his body improves. The child becomes more familiar with his own body and its capacities and limitations when he plays.

Intellectual Development

Successful adjustment requires the ability to adapt to change. With the challenges confronted in play the child tests and improves that skill: Climbing up the steps, piecing together a puzzle, coloring or painting a blank piece of paper in his own special way. As he meets and masters these obstacles he is "learning to learn", and developing skills for coping with life.

As the child repeats certain actions he becomes aware of consistencies in his experience: A ball thrown up into the air always comes down. These consistencies grow, and the child begins to build concepts.

Introduction To Physical Activities (Continued)

The actions of play help the child learn to think. His actions are gradually reduced in size and internalized until "he is able to do in his head what before he had to do with his hands". Instead of trying the square puzzle piece in several openings before fitting it into the square one, he can picture in his mind the square piece fitting into the square opening.

Social Development

In his play the child learns to get along with others: Sharing toys, helping a friend build a skyscraper with blocks, or collaborating in a very secret fantasy story. By observing the rules and boundaries set by himself, his playmates, and by adults the child gradually internalizes the rules and boundaries of his society, and they become a part of him.

Emotional Development

Play provides an acceptable avenue for the release of the strong emotions characteristic of early childhood. Many needs and desires not otherwise met are filled in play, helping to relieve some of the frustrations of life. If something, or someone, causes the child to feel fear, anger, or jealousy, he can play himself into the emotion-provoking role and reduce and gain control over it.

Personality Development

Just as play is important to each spoke on the wheel, so too it is the essential force in the development of the young child's total personality. Play provides the child opportunities to confront and overcome challenging situations. Positive experiences of successful mastery of his body, his emotions, and his environment contribute to a strong self-image.

In an article entitled, "Play in Personality Development", philosopher Lawrence Frank expresses his belief that by adequately providing play opportunities for a young child we can give him, "what will enable him to mature and face life with courage, confidence in himself and the adequacy he can develop for participating in social order".

Introduction To Physical Activities (Continued)

One basic task, then, of those concerned about the development or children between the ages of two and six is to facilitate the growth of their self-confidence in their ability to successfully master their environment. Providing a wide variety of play experiences is a reliable means to that end.

The play of young children is manifested in many forms: Dramatic play, imaginative play, symbolic play, physical play. The spontaneous, unfettered movement of *physical play* is an important facet of the child's life. "Only if a child can move freely," writes Lorena Porter, "is he able to learn about himself and his world."

Children do not acquire new skills or knowledge by sitting still and watching or listening to someone else. They need to be acting, to be moving, climbing, touching, falling, running, rolling, jumping, crawling, slipping, throwing, holding, hopping.

It is helpful to understand the feeling of *disequilibrium*, or the condition of imbalance, created by physical play. The "loss of poise" accompanying disequilibrium has the very important consequence of "preparing the child for maintenance of self-control in later life". Spinning like helicopters, walking the balance beam, or falling down on top of other children are ways that children put themselves into states of disequilibrium just for the fun of it.

Physical play provides opportunities for practice of many basic developmental skills that are not present in other forms of play.

It is necessary to recognize that physical play has value for a structured program of early childhood education. Many different types of play experiences are essential to the young child in developing the ability to adapt to the changing realities all around him. He learns about himself, about his environment, and about how to live with others when he plays.

Understanding the value of physical play is a first step toward implementing it as a regular part of the preschool curriculum. Physical play contributes an ingredient to the process of learning about life that no other play form does. The child's increasing control and coordination of his body is accompanied by the positive success experience of mastering physically challenging situations.

Physical Activities

Running Jumping Climbing Balancing Playing

<u>Skills To Develop</u>

- Self confidence
- Building physical strength
- Coordination

- Expressing Idea and Developing Imagination
- Balance

<u>Activities - Overview</u>

Climbing; Running
Walking - heel-toe; Climbing; Jumping rope; Throwing a ball
Activity and Movement Games

Balance Beam

<u>Equipment:</u>

Balance Beam, Jump Ropes, Balls, Bean Bags.

<u>Objectives:</u>

- Grow physically:
  - What I can do with my body;
  - Where my body can move comfortable (Examples: Limits - Safety)
  - How I can develop my abilities to achieve my ends; (Example: Practicing throwing a ball may result in enjoying playing catch, ...).

- Growth inside:
  - Sharing space;
  - Cooperating with others;
  - Expressing my ideas;
  - Listening to others;
  - Confidence in myself.

Physical Activities

Ideas for Outside Activities: Physical Activities

Race Area (in yard);   Climbing Situation;   Balance Beam;

Cleared dirt or grass area

1. Small Wooden Frame Climber
2. Hills, Trees

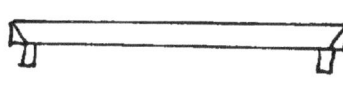

Ideas for Inside Activities:

Balance Beam;   Group activities in movement;

Teacher
(children in circle)
Gathering Time

Good Times for Physical Activities
Mid-Morning
Mid-Afternoon

More Activities:

- Soccer – outside team sport: Two teams. The object is to kick the ball into the other team's small net area at the opponent's end of the field. Equipment needed: One ball; Two portable net areas set up at each end of the field.

    Net Area made with Net nailed to standing boards.
    Size: About 5 feet high, 5 feet wide, 3 feet deep

- "Potato Sack" Races: Child puts both legs into a potato sack (burlap). He or she holds the sack up over the legs with both hands,...hopping across the race area to the finish line;
- Circle Games: Can be played inside or outside. Examples: "Duck, Duck, Goose", or "Ring Around the Rosie".

More Physical Activities

1. <u>Basic Body Movements – Walking (one foot off the ground at a time):</u>

    ⇨ Move forward around the room, without touching anyone else; Move fast, then move slow;

    ⇨ Walk forward/backward around obstacles and barriers;

    ⇨ Walk around shapes, letters, numbers drawn on floor;

    ⇨ Move backward, without touching anything or anybody; Move fast, then move slow;

    ⇨ Move forward, with eyes closed and arms extended in front, then above, out to sides, behind, on head, etc.;

    ⇨ Move from a squat with hands holding ankles (duck-walk);

    ⇨ Creative interpretation of animal walks, happy walk, sad walk, etc.;

    ⇨ With a partner, two legs tied together; Forward, backward, to the side, etc.

    ☺ <u>Skills:</u> Listed at front of Physical Activities Section.

    ✄ <u>Materials To Be Used:</u> Your Body; Obstacles; Barriers.

    ✎ <u>Teacher's Notes:</u> Discussion on results of activity; open format; Teacher records own results.

More Physical Activities

2. <u>Basic Body Movements – Running (two feet off the ground at a time)</u>:

    ⇨ Move fast, then slow;
    ⇨ Run backward;
    ⇨ Run, but stay in one place;
    ⇨ Run, turning in circles;
    ⇨ Run in a squat position;
    ⇨ Run and leap over a barrier;
    ⇨ Run, holding hands with partner; Forward, backward;
    ⇨ Run as if you are an animal; You are late; You are being chased; etc.
    ⇨ Run, stop, run.

☺ <u>Skills:</u> Listed at front of Physical Activities Section.

✂ <u>Materials To Be Used:</u> Your Body; Obstacles; Barriers.

✎ <u>Teacher's Notes:</u> Discussion on results of activity; open format; Teacher records own results.

More Physical Activities

3. <u>Basic Body Movements</u> - <u>Jumping (two feet off the ground)</u>:
   - <u>Hopping (one foot off the ground)</u>:

   ⇨ While clasping hands;
   ⇨ While turning in circles;
   ⇨ Jump (Hop), touch floor, jump (hop);
   ⇨ Sideways across the room;
   ⇨ Frontward across the room;
   ⇨ Backward across the room;
   ⇨ Jump down to floor from bench, or chair, or _____;
   ⇨ Jump higher than _____;
   ⇨ Jump rope;
   ⇨ Jump up and down with a partner;
   ⇨ Jump up and down holding partner's hand, or hands;
   ⇨ Jump over obstacle;
   ⇨ Jump like a _____.

☺ <u>Skills:</u> Listed at front of Physical Activities Section.

✄ <u>Materials To Be Used:</u> Your Body; Obstacles; Barriers.

✎ <u>Teacher's Notes:</u> Discussion on results of activity; open format; Teacher records own results.

More Physical Activities

4. <u>Basic Body Movements - Balancing</u>:

    ⇨ Stand on one foot, hands on head, hands on waist, hands out to side, one eye closed, two eyes closed;

    ⇨ Walk a straight line - heel-toe, hands on head, hands on waist, hands out to side, one eye closed;

    ⇨ Balance object on head: walk, run, sit down, get up, turn around, without losing or touching object;

    ⇨ Balance object on other body parts; i.e., shoulders, elbows, back of hand, etc.;

    ⇨ Cross a balance beam walking heel-toe, not looking at feet;

    ⇨ Cross a balance beam walking heel-toe; step over obstacle half-way across beam;

    ⇨ Cross a balance beam walking heel-toe; pick up object half-way across beam; walk the rest of the way;

    ⇨ Walk sideways across balance beam;

    ⇨ Walk backwards across balance beam;

    ⇨ Walk with hands on head across balance beam;

    ⇨ Walk, squat, walk across balance beam;

    ⇨ Walk, little jump, walk across balance beam.

☺ <u>Skills:</u> Listed at front of Physical Activities Section.

✂ <u>Materials To Be Used:</u> Balance Beam; Your Body; Obstacles; Barriers.

✎ <u>Teacher's Notes:</u> Discussion on results of activity; open format; Teacher records own results.

More Physical Activities

5. <u>Obstacle Course:</u>

To set up an obstacle course you take whatever you have around you and place it so that the children have to go under, over, around, behind, in front of, or through; and where the children have to walk, run, jump, hop, turn, crawl, climb, throw, catch, etc. The point of an obstacle course is to get the child moving, walking, catching, etc., in every way the Teacher can imagine, but it not only involves movement. It involves eye-hand coordination, spatial judgement, agility, body awareness, place-in-space awareness, balance and coordination. An obstacle course can be anything you can dream up, so use your imagination! You will find yourself enjoying the creativity of the set-up as much as the children enjoy using it.

⇨ Something to go over;
⇨ Something to go around;
⇨ Something to go over, under, around, through;
⇨ Something to jump over, down from, through;
⇨ Something to run around;
⇨ Something to throw over, through;
⇨ Something to crawl over, through, around;
⇨ Something to hop on, over, around, through;
⇨ Some pattern to copy; i.e., two hops, a jump, a step and a hop, etc.;
⇨ Something to climb up, down, around, laterally;
⇨ Something to balance on;
⇨ Use your imagination!

☺ <u>Skills:</u> Listed at front of Physical Activities Section; also see above.

✂ <u>Materials To Be Used:</u> Your Body; Obstacles; Barriers; Imagination!

✎ <u>Teacher's Notes:</u> Discussion on results of activity; open format; Teacher records own results.

More Physical Activities

6. <u>Ball Play:</u>

    ⇨ Bounce and catch ball;
    ⇨ Bounce, clap, and catch ball;
    ⇨ Bounce ball with two hands;
    ⇨ Bounce ball with one hand;
    ⇨ Bounce ball to partner;
    ⇨ Bounce ball, turn circle, catch;
    ⇨ Bounce ball, leg over, catch;
    ⇨ Sit on ground, legs apart, with partner, feet touching partner's; roll ball back and forth;
    ⇨ Roll ball completely around torso without dropping;
    ⇨ Stand with back on partner's back; pass ball back and forth at waistline in a circle around both partners;
    ⇨ Throw ball into hoop/bucket/basket;
    ⇨ Sit on floor; dribble/bounce ball continually as you rise to feet;
    ⇨ Play catch with a partner, trying not to let the ball touch the ground;
    ⇨ Play catch with a partner, using head to hit ball;
    ⇨ Play catch with a partner, using feet to hit ball;
    ⇨ Play team sports with ball; i.e., basketball, soccer, etc.;

☺ <u>Skills:</u> Listed at front of Physical Activities Section.

✂ <u>Materials To Be Used:</u> Your Body; Various sized balls; Hoops, buckets, baskets.

✎ <u>Teacher's Notes:</u> Discussion on results of activity; open format; Teacher records own results.

More Physical Activities

7. <u>Bean Bags (A small cloth bag filled with beans/rice)</u>:

   A.. <u>Tossing Activities:</u>

   ⇨ Toss upward and catch with one hand, both hands, back of hands. Attempt from both sitting and standing positions;
   ⇨ Toss overhead from one side to the other; from sitting and standing positions;
   ⇨ Toss overhead, turn and catch;
   ⇨ Toss upward, turn completely around and catch;
   ⇨ Toss upward, touch the floor and catch;
   ⇨ Toss upward, clap hands and catch;
   ⇨ Toss upward, clap hands behind back and catch;
   ⇨ Toss up and forward, run and catch;
   ⇨ Toss overhead, catch with hands behind back;
   ⇨ Toss from hands behind back overhead to front;
   ⇨ Toss around the body, under the leg, back hand behind the back, etc., and catch;
   ⇨ Lying on the floor, attempt the following:

   ⇨ Toss bean bag to self from various arm positions (above head, straight out at sides, below waist);
   ⇨ Toss bag to self from toe, then from both feet;
   ⇨ Using both feet bring bag overhead and deposit behind head; try to bring it up and put it down to side of body;
   ⇨ Standing, throw bag into air, sit down quickly and catch it;
   ⇨ Sitting, toss bag up, stand up and catch;
   ⇨ Try to juggle with two beanbags.

   B. <u>Feet Activities:</u>

   ⇨ Balance bag on instep and walk, then hop;
   ⇨ Swing leg forward and back with bag balanced on instep;

More Physical Activities

B. <u>Feet Activities (Continued):</u>

- ⇨ Toss to self from the toe, from knee, from heel;
- ⇨ Place bag between feet and jump several times;
- ⇨ Place bag between feet and toss to self;
- ⇨ Place bag on both feet and toss to self.

C. <u>Balancing Activities:</u>

- ⇨ Balance Beanbag on your head;
- ⇨ Walk, run, skip, hop, jump without losing the bag;
- ⇨ Sit down, get up; lie down, get up to a standing position;
- ⇨ Balance bag on other body parts (shoulder, elbow, back, hand) and try the previous activities;
- ⇨ Cross the balance beam with bag on head, on shoulder, on elbow, on your back.

D. <u>Partner Activities:</u>

- ⇨ Toss back and forth with different types of throws (one hand, other hand, under leg, around back);
- ⇨ Toss to partner with feet, both feet, toe;
- ⇨ Toss to partner with bag on elbow, head, knee;
- ⇨ Partners sit cross-legged about 10 feet apart; throw and catch in various ways.

☺ <u>Skills:</u> Listed at front of Physical Activities Section.

✄ <u>Materials To Be Used:</u> Your Body; Bean Bags.

✎ <u>Teacher's Notes:</u> Discussion on results of activity; open format; Teacher records own results.

www.fortheloveofchildrenbook.com   E-mail: info@fortheloveofchildrenbook.com

Part 10

Preschool Activities As Fundraisers

Preschool Activities Used as <u>Fun</u>draisers

In Preschool Activities
    Used as <u>Fun</u>draisers
        We use all
            Our talents
                As business
                    Trailblazers;

And create ideas
    We're intending
        To sell;
            Sharing things
                That we've made
                    And making money
                      As well!!

                              Vanessa Conaway Pace

Preschool Activities As Fundraisers

*Fun*draisers can be held at your school or at the Marketplace. A simple table or booth set up to display the projects your class has made would attract many. And the funds raised from the sale of these handmade items can be used to purchase needed supplies for your classroom.

Let the people know *why* you are selling your projects, and encourage them to buy.

Both children and adults can work together to set up the booth and sell the products.

Garden Projects

Weaving Work

Clay Art

Music Programs

Drama Programs

Puppet Art

Preschool Activities As <u>Fund</u>raisers

1. <u>Miniature Garden Indoors:</u>

   You can make a garden in a box.

   ⇨   Put stones in the bottom of the box.
   ⇨   Put soil on the top of the stones.
   ⇨   Plant seeds or small plants. Soon they will grow.
   ⇨   If you want a little "pool" in your garden take a jar lid, place it upside down in the soil and fill it with water to make a little pond. Place little rocks around the lid for decoration.

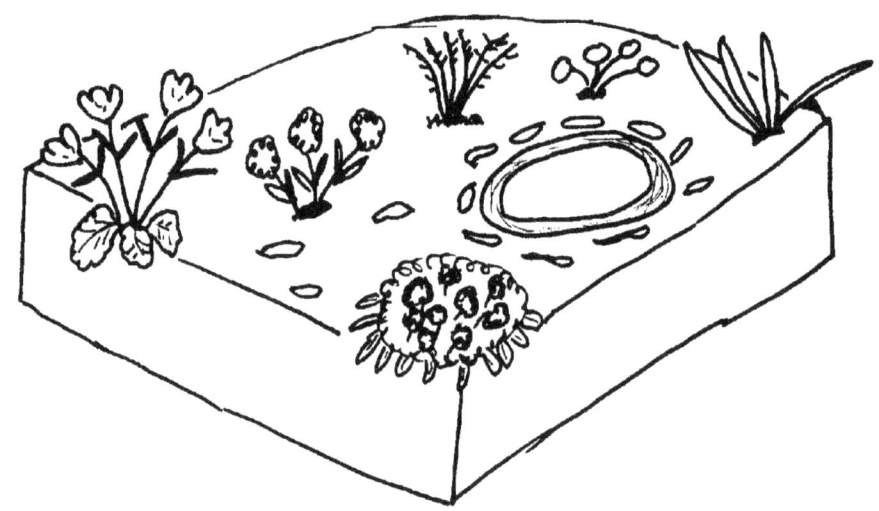

✂ <u>Materials To Be Used:</u> Wooden Box or Small Wooden Container; Seeds and/or Small Plants/ Grass Seed; Rocks; Lid from a Jar.

✎ <u>Teacher's Notes:</u> Discussion on results of activity; open format; Teacher records own results.

Preschool Activities As <u>Fundraisers</u>

2. <u>Growing Fruit Seeds</u>:

   ⇨ Gather jars or paper cups to use as pots;
   ⇨ Decorate them with collages made with paste and paper; or,
   ⇨ Color or paint the pots; or,
   ⇨ Mold pots from clay and bake them;
   ⇨ Plant some fruit seeds in flower pots;
   ⇨ Keep soil damp;
   ⇨ Small plants will begin to grow.

✂ <u>Materials To Be Used:</u> Pots made out of jars or paper cups, or molded from clay and baked; Soil; Small Stones; Fruit or Vegetable or Flower Seeds.

✎ <u>Teacher's Notes:</u> Discussion on results of activity; open format; Teacher records own results.

Preschool Activities As <u>Fundraisers</u>

3. <u>"Egg" Container Garden:</u>

   ⇨ Fill an empty egg container with soil (You may want to fill every other spot or cut the sections apart.);
   ⇨ Plant seeds or small plants in the soil areas
   ⇨ Do not let the soil get dry.
   ⇨ Soon plants and flowers will grow!

✂ <u>Materials To Be Used:</u> Egg Container; Soil; Seeds or Small Plants.

✎ <u>Teacher's Notes:</u> Discussion on results of activity; open format; Teacher records own results.

Preschool Activities As <u>Fundraisers</u>

4. <u>Plant A Large Garden:</u>

    ⇨ Have the children help with digging and planting, weeding and watering;

    ⇨ When vegetables and/or flowers are ready have the children decorate boxes or pots for the vegetables and flowers;

    ⇨ Sell them fresh from the "School Garden".

✂ <u>Materials To Be Used:</u> Seeds; Plants; Boxes; Pots; Decorate with Crayons, Paint, Paint Brushes; Collage with Colored Paper and Glue.

✏ <u>Teacher's Notes:</u> Discussion on results of activity; open format; Teacher records own results.

Preschool Activities As <u>Fundraisers</u>

5. <u>Soft Drink Stand:</u>

   ⇨ Gather supplies to make soft drinks; or,
   ⇨ Gather local fruits to make fresh fruit juices;
   ⇨ Find a good area where people will be passing by;
   ⇨ Set up a small wooden stand for displaying and selling the cold drinks and juices;
   ⇨ Help the children to sell the drinks.

✂ <u>Materials To Be Used:</u> Soft Drink Supplies; Fruits; Fruit Squeezer; Paper Cups; Small Wooden Stand for Selling Juice.

✏ <u>Teacher's Notes:</u> Discussion on results of activity; open format; Teacher records own results.

Preschool Activities As <u>Fundraisers</u>

6. <u>Weaving Placemats</u>:

   Children can weave simple place mats for the center of tables:

   ⇨ Use a colorful piece of paper 10" by 12";
   ⇨ Cut slits in rows across the paper;
   ⇨ Weave strips of paper in and out of the slits across the paper;
   ⇨ The Teacher prepares the paper and strips;
   ⇨ The child does the weaving;
   ⇨ Start with large slits and wide strips of weaving paper;
   ⇨ As the child becomes more proficient make the slits smaller and the weaving strips smaller.

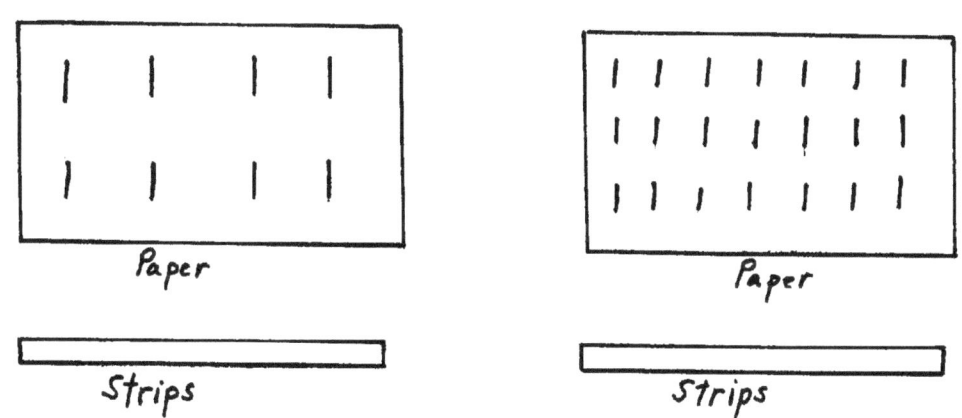

   ✂ <u>Materials To Be Used</u>: Colorful Construction Paper or Other Colorful Papers or Materials; Strips of Colored Paper for Weaving; Scissors.

   ✎ <u>Teacher's Notes</u>: Discussion on results of activity; open format; Teacher records own results.

Preschool Activities As <u>Fundraisers</u>

7. <u>Peg-Hand-Loom Hand Weaving</u>:

   ⇨ The children learn to weave on a small hand loom;
   ⇨ Looms can be made by an adult that is handy with wood;
   ⇨ Children age 5 or older can really enjoy this craft.
   ⇨ There are many different ways to weave a design:
      ⇨ A *"sampler"* – weaving a little bit of each design. Then you can pick the designs you like best for your next project;
      ⇨ A *"tapestry"* – A tapestry is a woven picture;
      ⇨ A *"wall hanging"* – Try weaving objects like beads, feathers, dried flowers, long grasses, or sticks into it;
   ⇨ The first step is to "warp" your loom. The warp is the white cotton string that you wind around the pegs:
      ⇨ Tie one end of the white cotton string to the first peg;
      ⇨ Loop the cotton string around each peg until you reach the other end;
      ⇨ Tie the string to the last peg;
      ⇨ Cut off any extra string;

 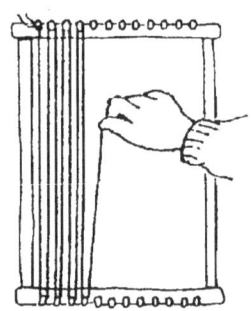 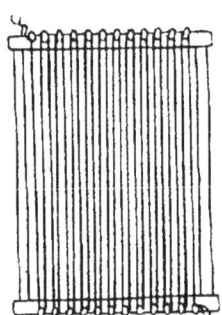

   ⇨ Then thread your needle;
   ⇨ Weave back and forth with the yarn doubled.

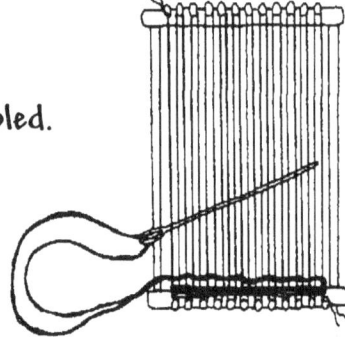

Preschool Activities As <u>Fundraisers</u>

7. <u>Peg-Hand-Loom Hand Weaving (Continued)</u>:

  ⇨ To do Plain Weaving:
  ⇨ Pass the needle over the first thread, then under the next – over and under – all the way to the end;
  ⇨ Pull the string or yarn all the way through, but leave a little tail hanging out, and tuck it in as shown in the diagram;

  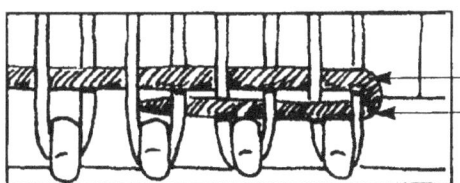

  ⇨ Tap the string or yarn down, as shown, with a fork or with your fingers;

  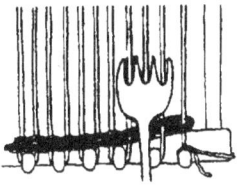

  ⇨ To weave Row 2 come back again, passing the needle *under* the first thread, and *over* the next – under and over – all the way to the end;

  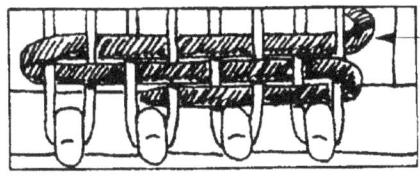

  ⇨ To weave Row 3 repeat Row 1, and then continue on with this pattern.

  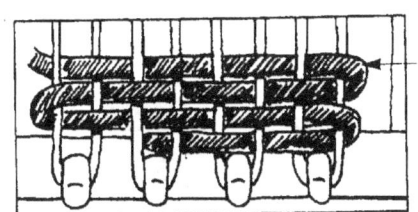

Preschool Activities As <u>Fundraisers</u>

7. <u>Peg-Hand-Loom Hand Weaving (Continued)</u>:

   ⇨ Try to keep the edges neat! It takes a lot of practice, so don't worry if they're not perfect;

   ⇨ Try new designs!
   - ⇨ You can make stripes from side to side:
     - ⇨ Weave one color for 3 or 4 rows;
     - ⇨ Cut the end (Remember to leave enough string or yarn to have a tail to tuck in!);
     - ⇨ Then weave 3 or 4 rows of another color;
     - ⇨ You can make the stripes as fat or thin as you like!

     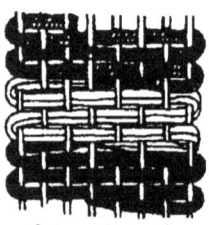
     Stripes side to side

   - ⇨ You can make stripes up and down:
     - ⇨ Try weaving one row of a dark color, like purple;
     - ⇨ Then weave the next row with a light color, like yellow;
     - ⇨ Do this several times and see what happens!

     Stripes up and down

   - ⇨ You can make holes or slits:

    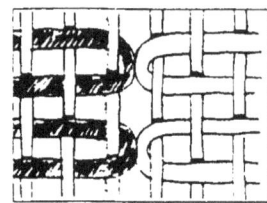

Preschool Activities As <u>Fundraisers</u>

7. <u>Peg-Hand-Loom Hand Weaving (Continued)</u>:

   ⇨ You can even weave a hill:

   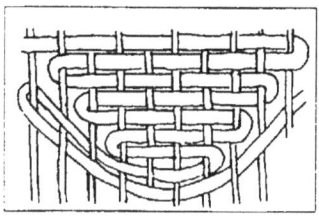

   ⇨ Or, you can do fluffy rya knots!

   ⇨ Finishing your Weaving Project:

   ⇨ Weave until you bump up against the pegs at the top of your loom;

   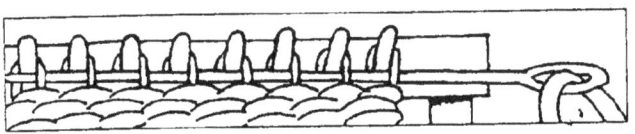

   ⇨ You can leave your weaving on your loom and use the loom as a frame for your weaving; or,

   ⇨ You can take it off by carefully pushing up from underneath your weaving to slide the strings off of the pegs;

   ⇨ If there is still a little room left to weave, do it;

   ⇨ Then cut your string or yarn and tuck in the tail;

   ⇨ Take the 2 warp ends that were tied to your loom and pull them back into the weaving with a small crochet hook or an unfolded paper clip;

   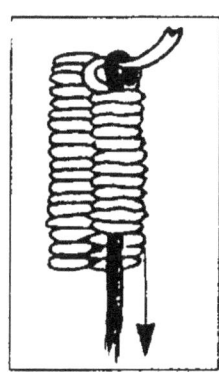

Preschool Activities As <u>Fund</u>raisers

7. <u>Peg-Hand-Loom Hand Weaving (Continued)</u>:

⇨ Ideas for projects and gifts:

⇨ You could weave a "tapestry":
  ⇨ Draw a simple picture of what you want to weave;
  ⇨ Tape the picture to the back side of your loom;
  ⇨ Then weave the design by looking at your drawing.

Note: You can make RYA knots (above) to make a sheep's body fluffy, if you want. You have to weave a row or two in between the rya to hold them in place.

⇨ Or, you could weave a purse:
  ⇨ Fold your weaving in half;
  ⇨ Sew up the sides.
⇨ Or, you could make a little pillow: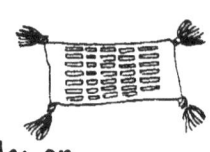
  ⇨ Weave two pieces;
  ⇨ Sew them together along the sides;
  ⇨ Fill the pillow with soft, fluffy materials; or,
  ⇨ Fill the pillow with sweet smelling herbs to be put in a bureau drawer to make it smell good.
⇨ Or, you could make place mats for the table;

⇨ Or, weave several pieces and sew them together for <u>mats for the children to sit on!</u>

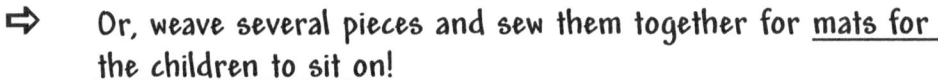

Note: Hand Weaving ideas and materials available from Harrisville Designs, Harrisville, New Hampshire 03450 USA.

✎ Teacher's Notes: Discussion on results of activity; open format; Teacher records own results.

Preschool Activities As _Fundraisers_

8. <u>Recipes For Classroom _Fun_ and _Fundraising_</u>:

Playdough (4 recipes)

1. 3 cups flour
   1 cup salt
   1 cup water with food coloring
   1 tablespoon oil

   Mix dry ingredients. Add water and oil gradually. Add more water if too stiff; more flour if too sticky. Let children help with the mixing and measuring. Alum may be added as a preservative, but is not essential in a cool climate.

2. 3 to 4 cups flour
   2 tablespoons cornstarch
   Food coloring
   1 cup salt
   1 cup warm water

   Sift flour and cornstarch together several times. Add the coloring and salt to the water. Gradually add this to the flour. Knead as for bread. Store in an earthen jar or large-mouthed glass container. Use enough coloring to give a full, rich color.

3. Uncooked Playdough

   1 cup cold water
   1 cup salt
   2 teaspoons cooking oil
   3 cups flour
   2 tablespoons cornstarch
   Powdered paint

   Mix the water, salt, oil, and enough powdered paint to make a bright color. Gradually work flour and cornstarch in until it is the consistency of bread dough.

4. Cooked Playdough

   1 cup salt
   1 cup water
   ½ cup flour

   Mix ingredients together and cook over medium heat. Remove from heat when mixture is thick and rubbery. As the mixture cools, knead in enough flour to make the dough workable.

Preschool Activities As _Fundraisers_

8. <u>Recipes For Classroom Fun and _Fundraising_ (Continued)</u>:

Cornstarch Clay

½ cup cornstarch   1 cup salt   ¼ cup cold water

Mix salt and cornstarch and cold water in upper part of double boiler. Stir mixture constantly as it thickens into a solid mass, about the consistency of bread dough. Place on aluminum foil or waxed paper to cool. Knead like dough. If it appears sticky, it needs a longer time over the heat, but it can be air dried before wrapping. It is now ready to use, or it can be stored for several days if carefully wrapped. If it has been stored for several days it can be kneaded before using.

Baker's Clay (Can be used for _Fundraiser_ Projects!)

4 cups unsifted all-purpose flour   1 cup salt   1 ½ cups water

Combine ingredients in a bowl. Mix thoroughly with hands. Knead from 4 to 6 minutes. Shape into shapes for decorations by hand or with cookie cutter. Cut holes with plastic straws if needed. Bake in 350° oven for 1 hour, or until lightly browned. When cool, paint with tempera or acrylic paints.

Modeling "Goop" (Can be used for Fundraiser Projects!)

2 cups salt   1 cup cornstarch
2/3 cup water   ½ cup cold water

Stir salt and 2/3 cup water over heat 4-5 minutes. Remove from heat. Add cornstarch and cold water. Stir until smooth. Cook until thick. Store in plastic bag. This may be used for modeling and will not crumble when dry, as some modeling clay products tend to do when unfired.

Craft Clay (Can be used for Fundraiser Projects!)

1 cup cornstarch   2 cups baking soda (1 lb. box)
1 ¼ cups water

Combine all ingredients and cook until thickened to dough-like consistency. Turn mixture out on pastry board and knead. Cover with damp cloth or keep in plastic bag. Good for plaques and other "models" which can be painted when dry.

Preschool Activities As *Fundraisers*

8. <u>Recipes For Classroom Fun and *Fundraising* (Continued)</u>:

   Salt Dough (Can be used for *Fundraiser* Projects!)

This dough is good for making beads, decorations and ornaments which can be painted or lacquered.

4 cups salt   3 cups water   2 cups cornstarch

Mix all ingredients and cook over medium heat, stirring constantly, about 3 minutes. Mixture should resemble the consistency of bread dough. Pour onto waxed paper. When sufficiently cool to handle, knead for a few minutes. Keeps well in plastic bag for 2 to 3 days. Salt dough dries very hard, and does not crumble. *Wouldn't this project be good for a fundraiser?*

   Chinese Dough (Can be used for *Fundraiser* Projects!)

This dough has a lovely translucent appearance, and takes either food coloring or powdered paint well. It is malleable, and can be worked into thin, delicate forms. It will retain its shape without shrinking, and dries to a tough, hard consistency without crumbling.

3 ½ cups flour   1 ¼ cups boiling water
1 ½ cups sweet rice flour*   4 teaspoons honey
7 teaspoons salt   *(also known as glutinous rice flour)

Mix both kinds of flour and salt in a large mixing bowl. Add 1 ½ cups boiling water and work the liquid well into the flour. Gradually add ¼ to ½ cup more water as needed to make a dry dough mixture. The dough should stay together, but not be sticky. Flatten dough into lump and steam for 30 minutes. Remove and break into smaller pieces and place on a rack or towel to cool. Knead in 4 teaspoons honey a little at a time, and add food coloring or powdered paint. Work into the dough. Mixture keeps well in a plastic bag, or keep a damp towel over the dough.

To make ornaments from Cornstarch Clay, Modeling "Goop", Craft Clay, Baker's Clay, or Chinese Dough:

1. Roll out the clay; cut out figures or designs with cutters;
2. Poke a hole near the top with a straw or pencil;
3. Bake at 225° for 2 hours, turning 3 or 4 times to prevent curling.
4. Color with tempera paints and glue on glitter or sequins.
5. Use ornament hooks, string, ribbon, or yarn for hanging.

Preschool Activities As <u>Fundraisers</u>

9. <u>Make Your Own Rock Candy</u>:

    ⇨ Tie a short piece of cotton string to the middle of the pencil or stick;

    ⇨ Attach a paper clip to the end of the string for a weight;

    ⇨ Moisten the string very lightly;

    ⇨ Roll the string in a bit of sugar (this will "attract" the sugar crystals from the syrup to the string);

    ⇨ Place the pencil or stick over the top of the glass or jar with the string hanging down inside;

    ⇨ Heat one cup of water to boiling, and dissolve 2 cups of sugar into it. For the biggest crystals FAST, heat the sugar-water a SECOND time, and dissolve as much additional sugar as you can into it;

    ⇨ Add a few drops of food coloring to the solution if you want colored candy;

    ⇨ Pour the solution into the prepared glass or jar and leave undisturbed for a couple of days.

    ⇨ Depending on how much sugar you were able to dissolve into the water, you should start to see crystals growing in a few hours to a few days.

✂ <u>Materials To Be Used:</u> 1 Glass Jar or Drinking Glass; 1 Piece of Cotton String; 1 Pencil or Stick; 1 Paper Clip; Food Coloring (optional); 1 Cup Water; 2 Cups Sugar; Additional Sugar.

✎ <u>Teacher's Notes:</u> Discussion on results of activity; open format; Teacher records own results.

Preschool Activities As <u>Fundraisers</u>

10. <u>Music and Drama Programs</u>:

    ⇨ Children and Teachers put together a show to entertain parents and others;

    ⇨ Charge a small fee for a *Fundraiser* project, maybe for new classroom books or games, or seeds for the garden.

✂ <u>Materials To Be Used</u>: Use your imagination!

✏ <u>Teacher's Notes</u>: Discussion on results of activity; open format; Teacher records own results.

Preschool Activities As <u>Fundraisers</u>

11. <u>Sock Puppets:</u>

    ⇨   You can make a puppet out of a sock;
    ⇨   Using your imagination, faces can be made out of paper or materials;
    ⇨   Sock fits over your hand.

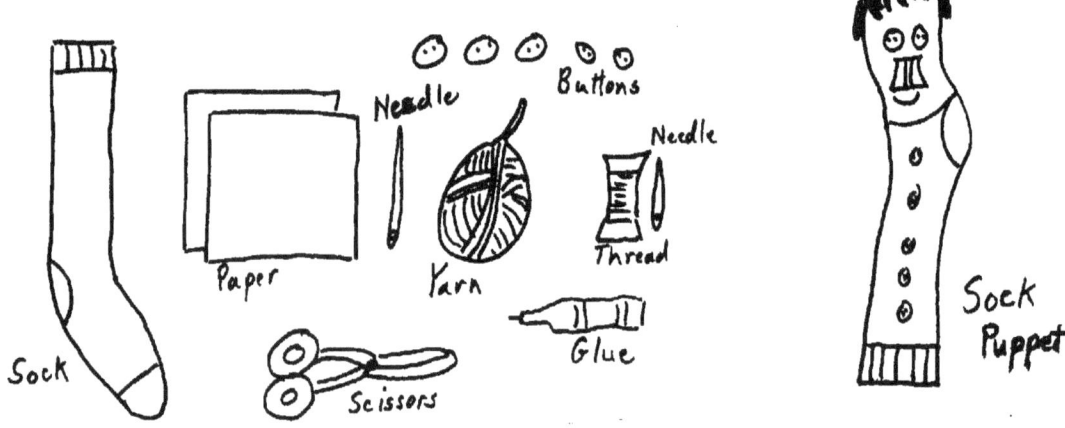

✂ <u>Materials To Be Used:</u> Socks; Colored Paper; Yarn; Buttons; Scissors; Glue; Needle and Thread.

✎ <u>Teacher's Notes:</u> Discussion on results of activity; open format; Teacher records own results.

Preschool Activities As <u>Fundraisers</u>

12. <u>Finger Puppets:</u>

    ⇨ These puppets fit over your finger;
    ⇨ At your Fundraiser Booth children can make their own puppet and buy it to take home with them.

✂ <u>Materials To Be Used:</u> Piece of Cloth; Rubber Band; Marker To Make Face and Clothes.

✎ <u>Teacher's Notes:</u> Discussion on results of activity; open format; Teacher records own results.

www.fortheloveofchildrenbook.com   E-mail: info@.fortheloveofchildrenbook.com

Part II
Preschool "Area" and "Floor Plan" Ideas

Preschool "Area" And "Floor Plan" Ideas

In Preschool "Area"
    And "Floor Plan" Ideas
        We find drawings
           That make
                Planning classrooms
                    A whizzzz!

Whether City
    Or Village
        Is your school's domain
           You can set up
              Your classroom
                  Without any pain!!

Vanessa Conaway Pace

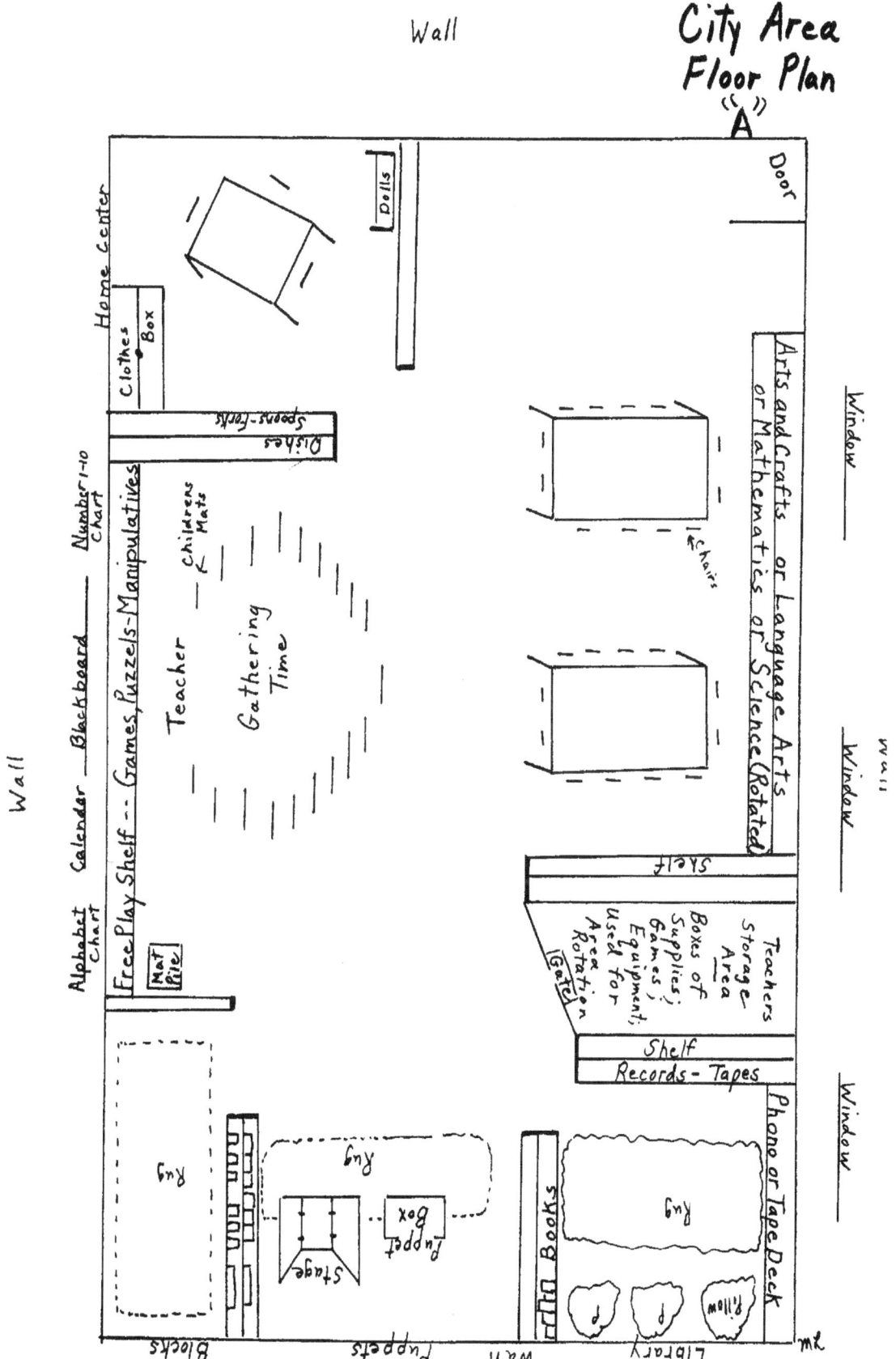

City Area Floor Plan

301

My Area and Floor Plans

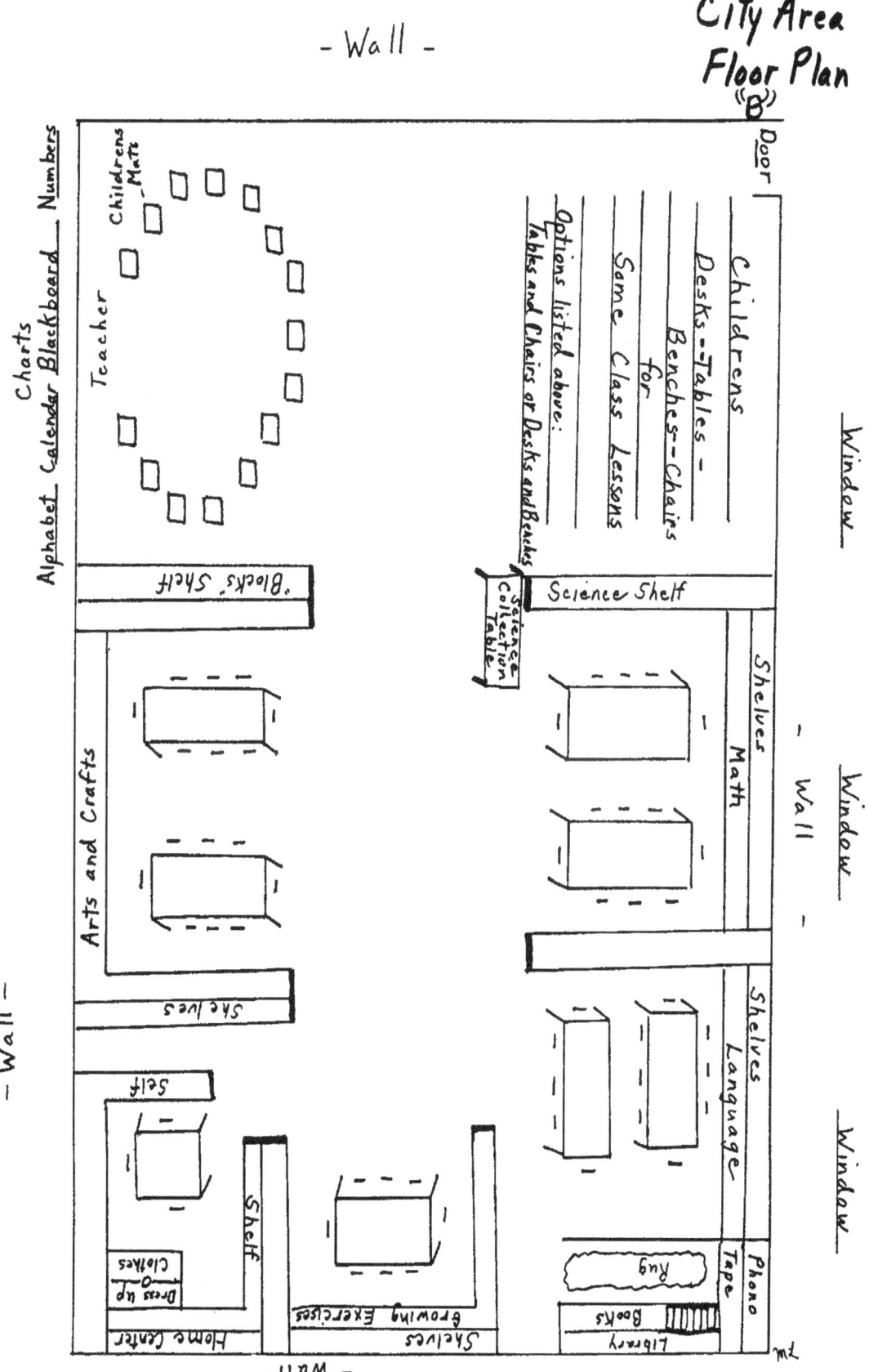

My Area and Floor Plans

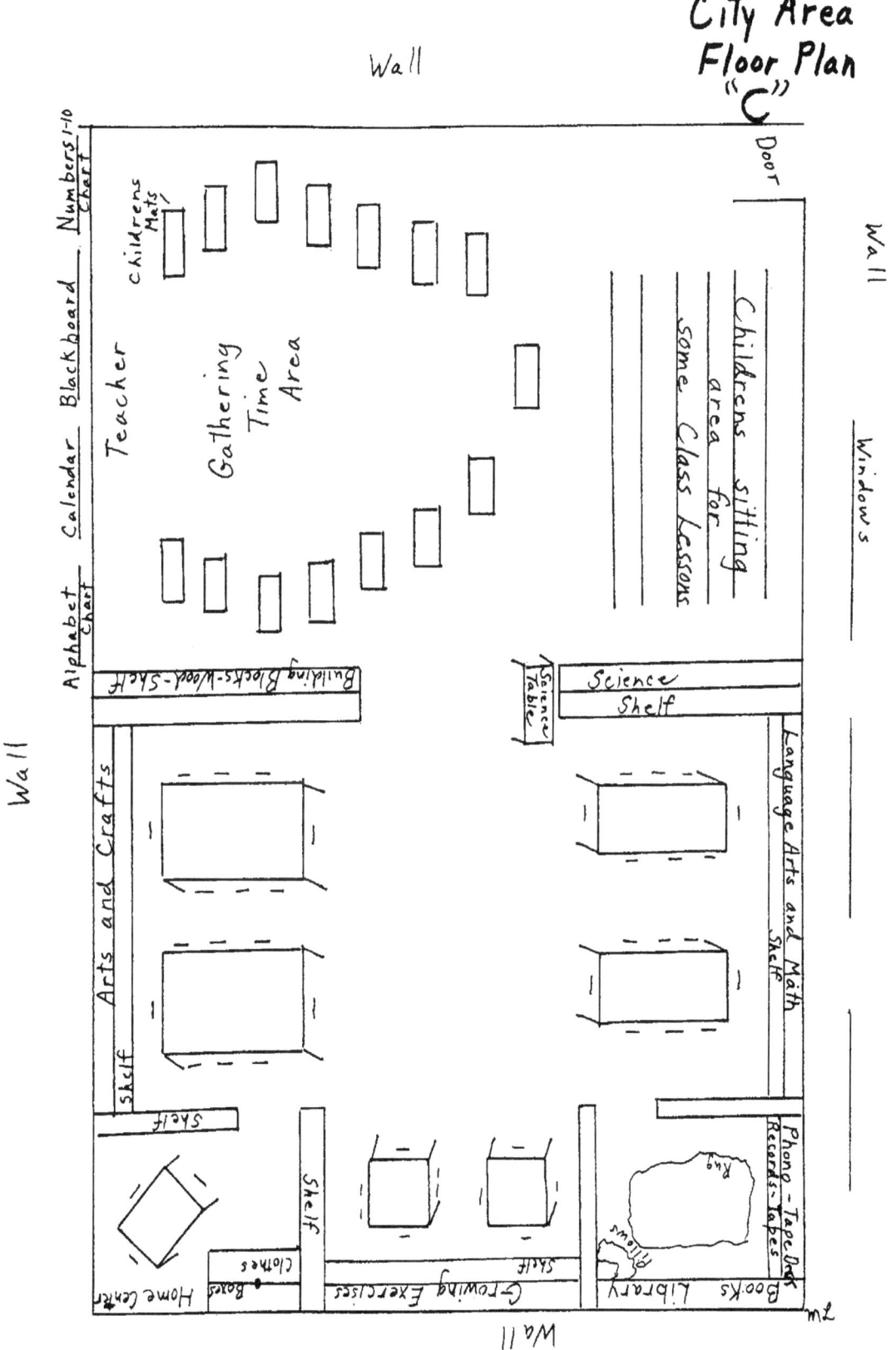

My Area and Floor Plans

www.fortheloveofchildrenbook.com   E-mail: info@.fortheloveofchildrenbook.com

Village Preschool Area

Arts and Crafts
Shelves
← Preschool Room
Inside Building Floor Plan ↓
Tables
Mathematics and Language
Science
Shelves

Preschool Building

Physical Activities

Blocks Games Puzzels
Tarp
Poles

Tarp
Poles
Gathering Time
Music, Stories
Creative Dramatics

The children can be rotated in small groups from the activities inside the preschool building to the activities outside under the tarps or in the school yard.
The number of tarp areas will depend on the number of children.

My Area and Floor Plans

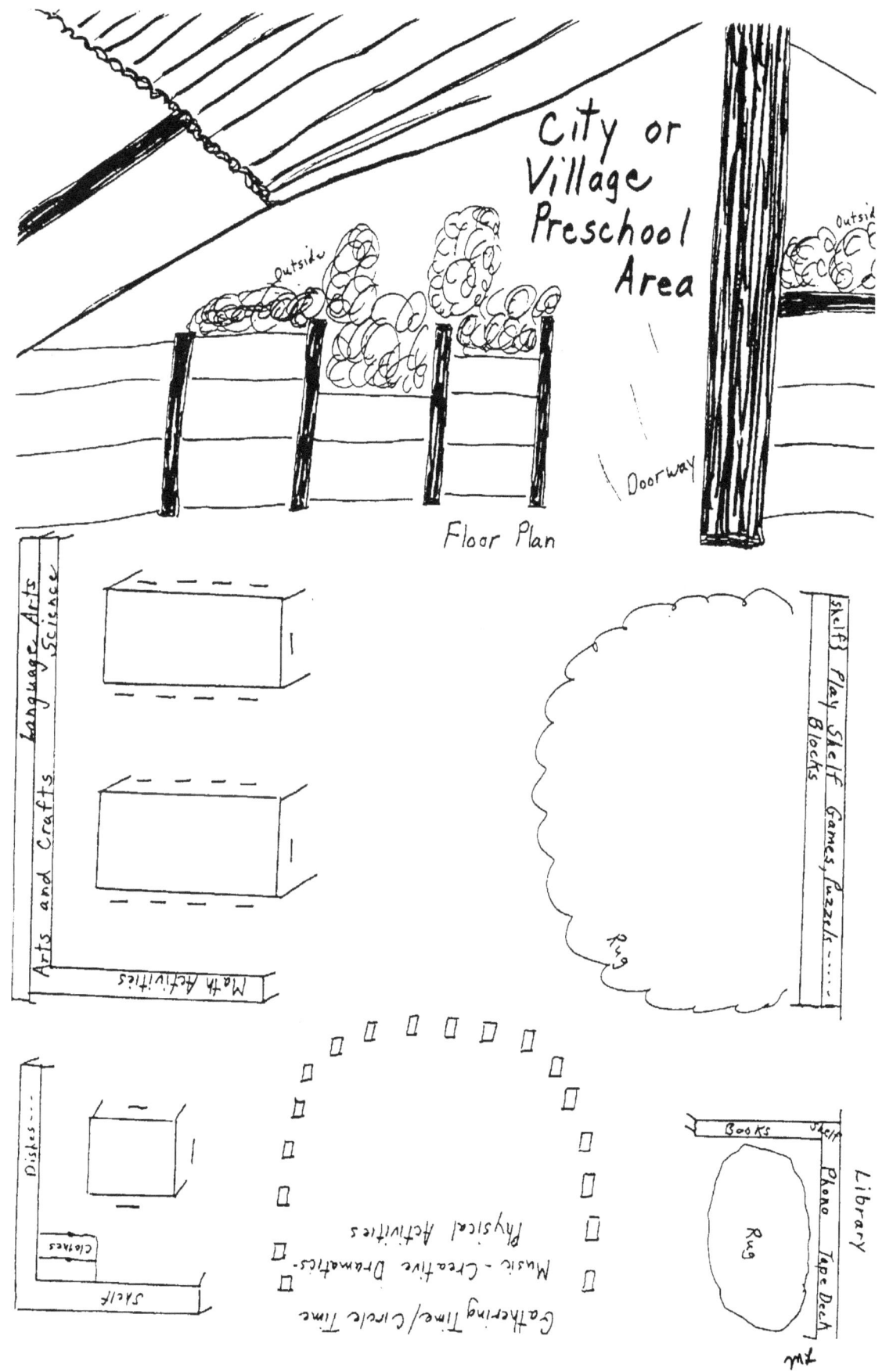

My Area and Floor Plans

www.fortheloveofchildrenbook.com   E-mail: info@fortheloveofchildrenbook.com

Readings List

Ames-Bates, Louise, and Ilg, Frances L.:
    Your Two-Year-Old; Terrible or Tender
    Your Three-Year-Old; Friend or Enemy
    Your Four-Year-Old; Wild or Wonderful
    Your Five-Year-Old; Sunny or Serene; Gesell Institute of Child
Development; Dell Publishing Company, Inc., New York, NY; 1979

Baratta-Lorton, Mary: *Mathematics Their Way* "Innovative Series"; Addison-Wesley Publishing Company, Inc., Menlo Park, CA 1976.

Beckman, Carol - Simons, Roberta - Thomas, Nancy: *Channels To Children, Early Childhood Activity Guide for Holidays and Seasons*; Published by Channels To Children, Colorado Springs, Colorado; 1982.

Burton, Leon and Hughes, William: *Music Play, Learning Activities For Young Children*; Addison-Wesley Publishing Company, Menlo Park, CA; 1979.

Children's Community Service Department: *Ring A Ring O'Roses*; Stories, Games, and Finger Plays for Pre-School Children; Flint, Michigan, 1977.

Colina, Tessa - Editor: *Finger Plays*, and How To Use Them; Standard Publishing Company, Cincinnati, Ohio; 1952.

Dallin, Leon & Lynn: *Heritage Songster*; Wm. C. Brown Company, Dubuque, Iowa; 1966.

Elikid, David: *The Harried Child; Growing Up Too Fast Too Soon;* Addison-Wesley Publishing Company, Menlo Park, CA; 1981.

Homfray, Margaret, and Child, Phoebe: *Children and Education;* Montessori World Education Institute.

Homfray, Margaret, and Child, Phoebe: *Practical Life;* Montessori World Educational Institute.

Homfray, Margaret, and Child, Phoebe: *Sensorial Education;* Montessori World Educational Institute.

Jenkins-Griffin, Peggy D.: *The Art of Puppetry;* A Guide for Those Working with

Young Children; Bellevue, Washington; 1971.

Ledbetter, Delores, Ed.: *Rainy Day Activities for Preschoolers*; Mercer Island (WA) Preschool Association; 1975.

Miller, Karen: *Ages and Stages; Developmental Descriptions and Activities Birth Through Eight Years*; Telshare Publishing Co., Inc., Marshfield, MA; 1985.

Miller, Karen: *Things To Do with Toddlers and Two's*; Telshare Publishing Col., Inc., Marshfield, MA; 1984.

Neubert, Ann Burke: *Montessori Everyday Life: A Way of Learning*; The Educational Book Publishing Division of The Early Education Company, Boston, MA; 1972.

Oesterreich, M.S., Lesia: *Ages and Stages*; Family Life Specialist, Human Devleopment and Family Studies, Iowa State University; www.nncc.org/child.dev/ages.stages.new.one.html.

Rogers, Cosby S., and Sawyers, Janet K.: *Play in the Lives of Children*; National Association for the Education of Young Children; Washington, D.C.; 1988.

Thompson, Myra K.: *Jump for Joy!*; Parker Publishing Company, Inc., West Nyack, NY; 1993.

Wirth, Marian Jenks: *Teacher's Handbook of Children's Games: A Guide to Developing Perceptual-Motor Skills*; Parker Publishing Company, Inc., West Nyack, NY; 1976.

Zink, Thomas C.: *The Learning Value of Physical Play for Preschool Children*; Downer's Grove, IL; 1973.

Zelmer, Usha Surya: Inner Preparation; Reporter 95; Fall 1995, Vol. XIX, No. 3.

Magazines

Ranger Rick: Published by National Wildlife Federation, Leesburg Pike, Vienna, VA.
Zoobooks; Wildlife Education: Published by Zoobooks, San Diego, CA..

ABOUT THE AUTHORS

The materials in "*For The Love Of Children: Guidebook for Early Education*" were compiled by:

Marguerite Laskares: 40+ years of experience as an Early Childhood/Primary Educator, Licenser, Establisher and Director of Preschools; B.S. Degree in Education from the University of Washington; Montessori World Educational Institute Teacher Trainer for Preschool and Primary Schools; Children's World Master Teacher Award; extensive continuing education courses; community services, lectures, and workshops in Early Childhood Education.

Tamra Pace: 13 years of preschool classroom experience and 4 years as owner/operator of her own Preschool; International Lecturer and Teacher Trainer in Early Childhood Education; Early Childhood Education Degree from North Seattle Community College, and extensive continuing education courses; community services, lectures, and workshops in Early Childhood Education.

Vanessa Conaway Pace: Teacher of the creative arts...voice and music; Managing Editor with more than 40 years of publishing and editorial experience; Author of a series of prose/poetry/music books with Kindle, cd's, and videos entitled "*Kaleidoscope: Life's Meaningful Reflections: Volume I: "That's ENUF!!!"; Volume Two: "One Great Gift"; Volume Three: "There's Greatness Within You"*. Two Long-Running Television Series Host, Producer, and Director; Recording Artist: Albums: "*He's ALIVE!!!*", "*Great Arias and Duets*"; Bachelor of Fine Arts Degree in Music Performance from Boston University, School of Fine and Applied Arts.

> Please see contact information
> for Lectures and Workshops available
> on the following page.

Pace Publishing International, Post Office Box 2187, Lynnwood, WA 98036
www.fortheloveofchildrenbook.com   E-mail: info@fortheloveofchildrenbook.com

CONTACT INFORMATION

"For The Love Of Children: A Guidebook For Early Childhood"

Workshops and Seminars

Please contact:

Pace Publishing International
Post Office Box 2187
Lynnwood, WA 98036

Website: www.fortheloveofchildrenbook.com

E-mail: info@fortheloveofchildrenbook.com

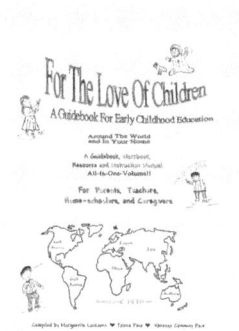

Request for Reader's Review

The materials in this all-inclusive "Guidebook" were compiled for the love of children and their caregivers! The book is circulating world wide, with positive results. Hopefully it is doing just that in your life! If this book has been helpful, useful, or enjoyable, in any way to you, or your children, or your loved ones, we would appreciate it if you would take a moment to write a review.

The Authors of this Guidebook,

and all the Teachers, Parents, and Caregivers

who are searching for these materials stated simply,

and in one convenient volume,

will Thank You!!!

For The Love Of Children: A Guidebook For Early Childhood (International Edition) Paperback – International Edition
by Marguerite Laskares (Author), Tamra Pace (Author), Vanessa Conaway Pace (Author)

Be the first to review this item

Please send reviews to the following link:

https://www.amazon.com/gp/product/1475210922?pf_rd_p=1cac67ce-697a-47be-b2f5-9ae91aab54f2&pf_rd_r=8T2ZA2MACC3A696WRC0H

Then scroll down near the end of the page and see "Write a Customer Review" link on the left.

www.ingramcontent.com/pod-product-compliance
Lightning Source LLC
Chambersburg PA
CBHW080304311025
34789CB00044B/3824